T0267104

FXCKBOYS ARE BORING

RYAN SHELDON

FXCKBOYS ARE BORING

A GAY MAN'S GUIDE TO DATING

for everyone

RISE
BOOKS

**RISE
BOOKS**

Cover design and illustrations by Vyana Novus
Jacket and interior design by Neuwirth & Associates, Inc.

Library of Congress Cataloging-in-Publication Data
Available Upon Request

ISBN 978-1-959524-03-8 (hardcover)
ISBN 978-1-959524-10-6 (eBook)

Printed in the United States of America
First Edition
10 9 8 7 6 5 4 3 2 1

This book is dedicated to those who have ever questioned their worth and felt they fell short of expectations. To anyone who has struggled with feelings of inadequacy and self-doubt, know that you are not alone. May these pages remind you that your uniqueness and imperfections are what make you human and that your journey to self-acceptance is a courageous and worthwhile journey. You are, and always have been, more than good enough.

CONTENTS

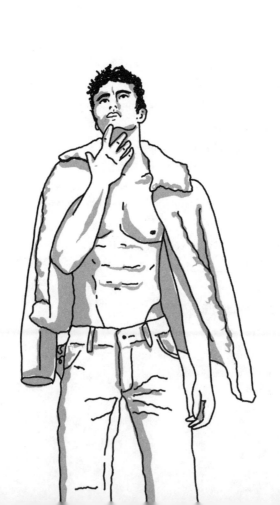

FXCKBOYS
ARE
BORING

PART ONE

SO MANY FUCKBOYS, SO LITTLE SELF-ESTEEM

INTRODUCTION

As I sat cross-legged, completely naked and unsatisfied, locked in uncomfortable and prolonged eye contact with a spiritual guru fuckboy, crystals of every shape, size, and color carefully positioned on the floor around me, I realized something. While this situation (along with many others I've had in my dating life) was unquestionably intriguing, I was once again in the same emotional position (albeit a different position physically)—I was trying to build a lasting, real, healthy relationship with a grown adult man, and he was trying to fuck me with a crystal.

After heading home again, disappointed, demoralized, and all-around d-bagged, I realized that I had not found love, as I had been hoping at the beginning of the date, but just another archetype for my Fuckboy Wall of Shame (yes, I have a wall, and yes, I'll be sharing it in this book). Whether you're gay, straight, bisexual, pansexual, or queer, chances are most of us in the dating world have encountered some type of fuckboy before.

What exactly is a fuckboy? The Urban Dictionary is a treasure trove of definitions for fuckboys. Here are a few of my favorites:

FUCKBOY
See also: dipshit
An asshole

A guy who uses someone
A guy who just wants sex
A guy who wants sex, not real love, out of a relationship
A guy who talks shit
A super shitty guy who people should avoid at all times

While I love all of these, my personal definition of a fuckboy is as follows:

FUCKBOY:
A chronically unavailable, dysfunctional, self-centered person who medicates with sex and control instead of being emotionally vulnerable and going to therapy to deal with their issues

While each dating experience I had with a fuckboy was unique, and sometimes downright disturbing, they all had the same boring similarities. They were predictable, selfish, and incredibly uninteresting. But they did provide me with a few things: hilarious, embarrassing, and sometimes cringeworthy stories for this book; lessons about how to love myself instead of seeking love in one-dimensional relationships; and the idea to create a compatibility scale based on lasting and meaningful traits rather than physical appearance.

Using this scale, I found my partner of two years, and we are still going strong. After years of focused effort of building a more healed relationship with myself, I discovered three things:

1. People will only love us to the extent that we love ourselves.
2. If I love myself, I don't have to subject myself to fuckboys ever again.
3. Fuckboys are boring.

As a gay man in Los Angeles who came out later in life (at age thirty, but that is *old* in gay years), as a brawny model who's been on billboards in Times Square and traveled the world, as a gay man who spent fifteen years dating women, and as an advocate speaking out about eating disorders among men, I've seen it all. Quick note for those of you who don't know what a brawny model is, it's a man with larger masculine features, like a football player. We're not exactly "plus-size," but we're larger models than those thin, chiseled Calvin Klein models.

My work as a brawny model allowed for me to travel the world and find all kinds of fuckboys across the globe. While I was navigating the absurd, heartbreaking, and hilarious adventures of dating in the modern world, I could have used a guide like this to help me avoid some major pitfalls and learn from those who survived. Now that I've come out of the trenches, I'm bringing gifts of wisdom (and some super salacious dating stories) for all. I have dated every kind of fuckboy. I'm sure some of my ghosts of fuckboy past will see this book and be terrified that I'm going to Taylor Swift them.

If you're one of those fuckboys, don't worry. I'm not here to expose anyone . . . except myself.

I've spent the majority of my life trying to achieve success, which to me meant having a perfect romantic relationship, a fabulous job, loving friendships, an amazing body, a beautiful family, tons of money, and a deep, genuine sense of happiness. Basically, I wanted a life that most of us are seeking—the kind of fulfillment at work and home that leads to joy. When it comes to love, however, my experiences had previously been far from joyous. My longest relationship, before I found my current partner, was with a woman. We were together for four years, and it was one of the most toxic, verbally and emotionally abusive relationships I've ever had. She often called me "worthless," "fat," "ugly," and the list goes on. I stayed for far too long because I was afraid of leaving, afraid that I wasn't going to find someone who accepted my body, afraid of being alone. I was terrified that I wouldn't find another person to fully embrace me. Looking back, my partner didn't even embrace me, and I certainly didn't accept myself.

By the time I came out as a gay man at thirty years old (like I said, *old* in gay years), I wasn't even sure what love and compatibility meant. I knew that I was attracted to men, but I was heavily influenced by my environment. I thought you had to be six feet tall with six-pack abs to even be considered fuckable. And as I began to date, I found out the belief in that lie was the norm for many of the men I encountered.

The toxicity that I had experienced in the straight world was downright endemic in the gay world—everyone seemed to be some type of fuckboy. But that's because I was overlooking substance and character for muscles and perfect teeth.

Fuckboys Are Boring is a guidebook for anyone out there who has ever struggled with feeling inferior, unworthy, or less than while trying to find love in this digital dating hellscape. For years, I looked for a book from a guy's perspective for dating in the modern world while living in a larger body. I needed a guide to help navigate all the weight discrimination, the nagging feelings of not being good enough, and the journey to feeling worthy of love while living within a prison of harmful social norms. But as they say, if you can't find the book, write the book. So, I'm inviting you into my story, which began with wild dating experiences but ultimately became about my relationship with myself. Perhaps if we all spent more time sharing our own personal stories of struggle then maybe, just maybe, we could break down the stigmas and finally learn to love ourselves authentically—not in the syrupy sweet way that marketing and social media have defined as self-love.

Most of us have experienced the sparks of a new relationship: the butterflies, the intoxicating uncertainty, the obsession over texts and social media posts displaying flawless bodies. But what if love, acceptance, and sex had nothing to do with six-pack abs and sparks at all? What happens after all those feel-good chemicals in our brain wear off and we're just two messy human beings trying to connect? What if we could redefine what true connection means in the first place? I spent my whole life believing that success and happiness couldn't be achieved unless I had all of these external things that proved my worthiness. I thought every box had to be checked, and when it wasn't, I found myself spiraling into a deep depression. I pushed myself to achieve an unrealistic level of success and find a fantasy romance like the ones in the movies, the flawless kind that our superficial society deems acceptable. It only took me thirty-three long years to finally understand that a fulfilling life is defined by me, not by anyone else, and that there aren't enough fuckboys in the world to bring me the fulfillment I'm seeking.

To be honest, I've been a fuckboy too. My fuckboy heyday is the stuff of legend. But I've also been in years of therapy to work through my issues. Not all fuckboys are bad people; they're just tragically boring. I don't mean that they aren't interesting people; they just refuse to grow—and that gets old real fast.

There are two types of fuckboys:

1. The Toxic Fuckboy—These fuckboys don't care whom they hurt, and they love creating drama and chaos (oh, how I used to *love* the chaos). Example: the fuckboy who plants seeds about your future together and intentionally strings you along (a.k.a. breadcrumbing), even though he has no intention of pursuing anything beyond a fling.

2. The Decent Fuckboy—This fuckboy isn't malicious; they just like booty calls with no strings attached. They'll tell you up front that they are interested only in hooking up and that you're free to leave if that's not your cup of tea. They say goodbye instead of ghosting, and they treat you with decency and respect during your short encounter.

It's all about intent. My boyfriend thought I was a fuckboy when we first met (which I was). It just so happened that I met him after I'd done enough healing and therapy to at least have an inkling that I wanted a more fulfilling relationship. Those two things, me meeting the man who would become my long-term boyfriend and being fed up with fuckboy life, came together at the perfect time, which allowed me to step out of Fuckboy Land and into a loving relationship.

The Compatibility Scale

But I didn't just slip and fall into a meaningful relationship. When I got sick of the same nonsense on repeat in my dating life, I collaborated with my therapist and created a compatibility scale, which I used to rate my dates according to the things that mattered most to me. I wrote down my values and deal-breakers, created a list of non-negotiables, and then rated each of my dates on a scale from 1 to 7 to determine how well they matched with my values in each category. It wasn't until I crafted this compatibility scale that I realized how little six-pack abs and a chiseled jawline mattered when it came to what I truly wanted out of a relationship. In this book, I'll share my personal compatibility scale (the one that led me to my long-term boyfriend) and help you create your own so you can venture into the dating world with a compass, knowing exactly what you want and with full knowledge of what you will and won't tolerate.

Through the course of my dating life, I've met the full spectrum of fuckboys, every type imaginable. Each fuckboy brought with them a lesson I needed to learn about myself. *Fuckboys Are Boring* will take you through the tales of the comically tragic fuckboys I've dated, what they taught me, and what being attracted to different types of fuckboys says about those of us in the dating world.

But this isn't just a catalog of salacious stories. I'll also share my struggles with binge eating disorder, which led me to become the chair of the Ambassador Program at the National Eating Disorders Association. I'll talk about the hard stuff, like overcoming OCD (obsessive-compulsive disorder) and getting out of an abusive relationship. I'll discuss the work it took for me to get to a place where I unapologetically accepted myself, including my imperfect body. When we unapologetically accept ourselves, the odds of getting crystal fucked by a spiritual guru fuckboy decrease significantly. I wish I could say that's the wildest story in this book, but as you'll soon find out, it's not even close.

Consider this a judgment-free zone for you to explore the adventures of Fuckboy Land and maybe get to know yourself a little better. In my opinion, everyone should date a man at least once to see how hard it is. Fortunately, I've dated every type of man, so you don't have to.

This book can be used for entertainment or educational purposes (or both).[1] It can also be used as a natural fuckboy repellent (trust me, when a fuckboy sees you casually reading this book on the beach, they'll turn around and walk the other way). If it doesn't repel the more persistent fuckboys, feel free to use this book as a weapon.

---

1 The stories you are about to read are true, only the names (and some identifying details) have been changed to protect the (not so) innocent.

It is important to note that this book isn't just for gay men, or people who date men. It's a book for everyone seeking solace from the highs and lows of dating in the modern world.

CHAPTER ONE

Modern Dating Is a Dystopian Hellscape

Has online dating and the constant busy-ness of the modern world killed romance? The answer is yes and no. The romance our parents or grandparents knew is long gone, and, for some aspects of that outdated patriarchal paradigm, good riddance. But the act of courting someone you met at an ice-cream social, walking them to the movie theater, and holding hands on the first date—that's history, and it's also kind of sad. Because instead we've replaced it with Tinder swipes, mind games, porn fantasies, and uncomfortable sex in a car after knowing each other for only a few hours.

Dating in today's society is like playing a game of Where's Waldo? We are tasked with an endless search for our Waldo: a normal human who shares our values, isn't creepy, and won't ghost us. But Waldo is almost impossible to find in a sea of instant gratification fuckboys. The harder we search, the more desperate we become, or the more appealing it becomes to remain blissfully single with a few house-plants and a brunch bestie to keep us company.

With all of the apps at our fingertips, I can't help but wonder, what if the technology that was designed to bring us together is actually pulling us apart? Gay psychiatrist and author of the Vox article "We Need to Talk About How Grindr Is Affecting Gay Men's Mental Health," Jack Turban called the app an "underground digital bathhouse" and found that some users are allured to it not by the rush to feel good but to stop feeling bad.

In a survey conducted by Turban, users told him that after they closed the app, they were left feeling more depressed and lonelier. And it's the same story for heterosexual dating app users. Singles Reports found that four out of five dating app users reported feeling emotional fatigue and burnout. It's a weird time to be dating in this everyone-at-your-fingertips, quick hookup, swipe-left-or-right, fuck-boy, ghosting digital hell. No wonder we're tired.

So how do we find our Waldo in this atmosphere? Well, we have to be able to spot the fuckboy pitfalls first. If we are to overcome the fuckboy, we must first understand the fuckboy. We must become familiar with their types, tactics, and tragic character flaws.

The Fetishizer Fuckboy

"I want to feed you jelly-glazed donuts as you bounce up and down on my dick." *Well, there are worse things*, I thought. It took only about twenty minutes into our first date for me to realize something was . . . off about this guy. I would later find out that he was a feeder-and-gainer fetish fuckboy. For those who don't know, a feeder and gainer is someone who gets off by watching people eat copious amounts of food and gain weight before their eyes. There's a whole porn thing about it.

I found this attractive guy on an app. At that time, my only deciding factor for compatibility was their level of hotness, so I met him for a date at a bar. He was even cuter in person. At first, we got along great. As I listened to him talk, I started emotionally masturbating, a thing I did often on dates when I would envision my entire happy, gorgeous life with him . . . when I've known him for all of five minutes. I did this a lot.

In fact, as soon as I swiped right on a guy, the emotional masturbation would begin. We'd be traveling the world, going to dinner parties, and crying in each other's arms after the most amazing sex ever in the house we bought together after a beautiful Victorian-style wedding where everyone dressed in pastel colors and did expertly choreographed dance routines to Katy Perry's "Teenage Dream" on the dance floor . . .

Wait a minute, what is he looking at? My dreamy future husband's eyes were glued to my stomach. It was hanging a bit over the waist of my pants.

"Is there something wrong?" I asked.

"Oh no," he said. "I just have to tell you that I am so attracted to you."

Oh, okay, this is great! I didn't really understand what was happening, but I was into it. After going to a few more bars, my date insisted that I order food. I politely declined, but he kept pushing.

"Do you want to order some wings?" he pressed.

"No, I'm good." I couldn't help but notice this strange look in his eyes. As the end of the night approached, he invited me to hang out in his car for a bit. Surely, we will have a life-altering connection in his car, like the ones they have in movies. This would be the moment that could change our lives forever.

"Okay, sure," I smiled (Victorian wedding, hot sex in every room of our French country home with a three-car garage because he just *loves* his woodworking hobby—wait, does he have any hobbies? Eh, I'll find out later). His car just happened to be parked next to a late-night fast-food burger restaurant. It was around 1:30 a.m., and the drive-through line wound all the way around the parking lot. We were making out when suddenly he started grabbing my stomach and pinching my fat. I was a bit confused but loving the attention.

"What's going on?" I stammered.

"You're so hot," he said. I looked down, and he had the biggest hard-on I've ever seen. Apparently, he was incredibly turned on by grabbing my fat. Then he started saying things like, "I want to feed you jelly-glazed donuts while you bounce up and down on my dick."

Okay, what! I mean who doesn't love a jelly donut, but this was not what I had in mind for our epic origin love story.

"I want you to wear a wrestling singlet while you stand on a scale," he panted. "I want to watch you eat oatmeal raisin cookies that I made for you and see the number go up on the scale as you eat."

Uh . . . what the fuck is wrong with this guy? I had no clue what the hell was happening. My woodworking future husband was suddenly grabbing my ass and saying, "Oh, it's like Jell-O." Wait, should I be offended by this? I was conflicted because he was comparing my butt to Jell-O, but I was oddly kind of into it. I couldn't tell if this was disrespect and degradation or the most aggressive display of body positivity I'd ever seen.

This is fine, I thought. *Isn't it?* After some fooling around and fogging up the windows, he asked me if I wanted a burger and then immediately broke down crying. He said it had been a year since he'd broken up with his boyfriend, and he hadn't been intimate with anyone since.

After he finished sobbing, I awkwardly squirmed out of his car. "Um . . . have a great night," I said.

You'd think that burger-donut-tear fest would've been the end of it, right? Nope! I wanted a connection so bad and felt so low about myself that I went home and googled what happened so I could understand him better. That's when I discovered this guy had a fetish called "feeders and gainers." I came across all of these porn sites with people grabbing stomachs and stuffing their faces, gaining weight on the spot, and moving the numbers up on a scale. I couldn't believe this was actually a thing.

At first, I felt neither bad for myself nor disrespected. I even sent him a video the next day of me eating a cookie. He texted me back acknowledging his obvious need for therapy, and we never saw each other again.

My straight therapist sat wide-eyed across from me, her pen poised above her notebook, in total shock when I told her about the Fetishizer Fuckboy. It was clear that she was way out of her depth on this one. After she picked her jaw up off the floor, she expressed deep concern for me. As far as I know, I was her only gay patient, and she'd never heard of anything like this before.

"Don't you feel disrespected?" she asked. I told her it just seemed like a fetish, so not really. Fetishes can be pretty common in the gay community, whether it's feeders and gainers, race stuff, daddy stuff, or being fetishized for being a bigger guy. For a long time, I didn't want to be a bear (a term in the gay community for larger, often harrier guys who are perceived as rugged and masculine). The more I thought about it and processed what happened, the more awful I felt. It was dehumanizing. I felt othered, like a reluctant novelty act in a sick circus I never agreed to join. There was resistance in me when it came to the subcultures of the gay community. Later, I thought maybe I should just own the way I'm perceived, bear, brawny, whatever. For me, it's important that I'm showing up as someone with agency instead of as an unwilling participant.

The fetish fuckboy was so strange to me, and I wasn't even into it. Yet I was willing to go out with him again because I was desperate for connection, and he was so good looking. He fit the bill of the "perfect guy" because all I was looking for was looks. Considering how much I was willing to overlook for this guy, I was stunned when he rejected me. The guy that wanted to get me in a wrestling singlet and watch me eat cookies on a scale told me he needed space.

The modern dating world is no place for the weak.

Dating Is a Mess Because People Are Messes

If you think about humanity as a whole, it's no wonder dating is so . . . complicated. Everyone is knocking around with all of these unhealthy ideas, tendencies, and behaviors. We're isolated and lonely, looking for someone who at least complements our crazy. Let's face it, we're all a little fucked up. We chase love, avoid love, or twist and distort love into fetishes and games. We are all desperate for connection, but we sabotage ourselves and, therefore, our ability to connect with others. We have become experts at reinforcing our barriers to love and genuine connection. And so, as a balm, we make up our own stories about whom we should love, how they should look, and what they can offer us.

If I had to pinpoint the moment my date with fetish fuckboy was doomed, it was long before he asked me to stuff my face with jelly donuts. We were doomed as soon as I started emotionally masturbating to a made-up version of the guy instead of paying attention to the complicated human being in front of me. I was willing to do whatever it took to fulfill my fantasy, even if it meant donning a wrestling costume and eating burgers on a scale.

Pia Mellody, author of *Facing Love Addiction*, has a profound philosophy on what I call "emotional masturbation." In her interview with Alanis Morissette, Mellody said that love addicts will objectify their love interests and not even see them as human beings. When we get caught up in the fantasy, we're not seeing the person, we're seeing only what we make up about them. She asserts that love addicts tend to be attracted to people who are love avoidant. This usually stems from childhood. For instance, if a child was emotionally neglected by their parents, they may feel compelled to seek love. If left unchecked this seeking can turn into love addiction in their adult relationships. If a child was enmeshed with their parent, they may become love avoidant in adulthood. So while it would seem that I was the only one being objectified by the fetish fuckboy, the truth is, we were both objectifying each other. I went out with him for his looks, not for him as a person. When things got weird, I tried to maintain the connection because of my fantasy of him, not because I saw something in him as a human being.

In addition to our dysfunction around love, our sense of connection is often barricaded by superficiality and lack of trust. In this society, we're taught that if we want to feel worthy and wanted, we must look a certain way. If we don't meet the visual standards collectively made up by society, we feel inferior, which makes us act inferior, which shows the world that we believe we're unlovable. People pick up on our insecurities and treat us the way we feel on the inside. Rejection and disrespect make us feel even worse about ourselves, and the cycle continues.

The unfortunate reality is that perceived attractiveness is connected to our livelihoods. Research confirms that we have a better chance of being hired if we're hot. Attractive people get paid more, by about 12 percent. In politics, the cuter you are, the more likely you are to get elected. It's called the "beauty premium" by psychologists. I call it total bullshit. We're all chasing after these measurements that someone else decided we must meet in order to be successful, well liked, wealthy, and so on. While juggling all the human complexities surrounding relationships, we are also constantly swallowing a cocktail of societal expectations and standards that make truthful, vulnerable human connection nearly impossible.

We live in a world that says we are lovable only if our faces are chiseled and symmetrical, if nothing is sagging or jiggling, if we have six-pack abs, perfect smiles, and rock-hard, ten-inch dicks or pristine, tight, well-manicured pussies. In a landscape of impossible standards, it's no wonder we are guarded and isolated.

Who wants to be soft and vulnerable in this mess? But what if we came up with our own measurements of worthiness instead?

A Sea of Swiped Faces

Online dating is a fairly new phenomenon. Our parents didn't have dating apps. They had to go out and meet people the old-fashioned way—face to face, at singles bars and roller-skating rinks. Now our entire romantic future is determined by whether or not someone swipes left or right on us. We've reduced ourselves to photos flying by in half a second. Perhaps I'm stating the obvious here, but there's something so cold and inhumane in these apps. I should know. I've spent countless hours on the apps, and ultimately I learned that I mean nothing to these people. I'm just another swipe.

If you're someone like me, who is drawn to the fantasy of a person, social media is the worst place to find love and connection. First, if we're scrolling and sliding into someone's DMs, chances are we're staring into that cold hard screen to soothe the sting of loneliness. Everyone is presenting a curated, fantasy version of themselves on social media, with filters, lighting, flattering angles, and lavish back-drops. We're not seeing the truth behind those posts. Yet we still buy into it all.

During the height of the pandemic, I remember scrolling through Instagram. I came across this extremely attractive guy, so I went onto his feed and scrolled through his posts. Suddenly, I felt this sinking feeling in my stomach. It was a familiar feeling, but this time, I examined it. What I discovered is that that sinking feeling was coming from comparison. As Iyanla Vanzant said, "Comparison is an act of violence against the self."

I didn't look anything like this Instagram hottie. He had abs that could grate cheese and hundreds of thousands of follows and likes. How could I possibly compete when my posts are only getting a few hundred likes and my abs look . . . nothing like that?

I felt sad that I would never be the boyfriend on his arm. Looking at his feed, I felt discouraged because I thought I would never have that many followers or likes, no matter how many hours I spent creating the perfect posts. Then it hit me. I could just unfollow this guy. In fact, I have the freedom to unfollow anyone who makes me feel like shit. This is true in the real world too. If someone is bringing you down, making you feel bad about yourself or the world, or add-ing negative value to your life, you can walk away. Why should we torture ourselves?

For some, dating apps are the beginning of a beautiful relation-ship. For others, dating apps are an endless pursuit of the perfect mate or moment. A study in the *Journal of Social and Personal Relationships* showed that some participants struggled with compul-sive use of dating apps. They felt more confident as their online per-sona versus their real-life selves. Some of the participants even admitted that they missed school, work, and social activities because of their use of dating apps.

It can be so intoxicating, scrolling through these apps and lubing up for another emotional masturbation session. I'd swipe right, we would match, and all of a sudden, I'd be swept up into a fantasy. Within seconds, we're spending the summer at his parent's lake house and celebrating Christmas in Paris, as a family. We'd fight only about the little things, retire in Italy, and die in our sleep at ninety-seven years old in each other's arms . . . oh wait . . . he's only five foot seven? Ew. Never mind. Swipe!

There is so little at stake for us and the person on the other end of the screen. We can easily dismiss, swipe left, or ghost for the most superficial reasons, like height. But in the digital dating age, everybody is swiping and ghosting. It's the name of the game and the opposite of personal.

I'm guilty of it too. When things become too real (apparently nobody can see the fantasy in my head and act accordingly), it's tempting to cut and run. I was hooked on the adrenaline rush of new dating relationships. But just like Leo DiCaprio's girlfriends, young relationships eventually age.

For a love addict like me, stable, long-term relationships don't hit the brain like a random weird encounter in the parking lot of a burger joint. The thrill was in the chase. If there was no chase, I'd lose interest. I started playing the game too, giving my dates nicknames instead of calling them by the name they gave on the app. This was my way of protecting myself from people who had no stake in the game of online dating. They had to earn their way out of the nicknames I gave them. If we met and there was a connection, I'd call them by their real name. Until then, they were the Fetishizer, Cocaine Cowboy, Mama's Boy, and so on. If they weren't real to me, their names wouldn't be real either.

Love In the Time of COVID

For me, the pandemic was fuckboy central, but it was also nice guy central. The age of COVID-19 was a bizarre landscape for dating. I was going on three dates a week, and the stakes were low. Instead of high-priced meals at fancy restaurants, we met over Zoom. And I wasn't spending hours trying to make myself attractive before dates. I relied on flattering lighting and camera angles to hide what I wanted hidden. This alleviated the stress of worrying that my date would see my fat rolls and reject me. Pandemic dating was all over the place. On my first pandemic date, we wound up naked in our beds. Then I had one guy show his asshole to the camera . . . because he thought that's what I wanted to see.

Still, there were other guys who seemed genuinely interested in starting a relationship. Jesse and I hit it off right away over Zoom. After a few months, we decided it was safe to meet in person without too much worry about catching COVID. We enjoyed a socially distanced dinner and had fun together. I thought we had a good connection. That is, until the next day, when he texted me to tell me that my neighborhood, Santa Monica, is too far away from him. If you live in L.A., you know that nobody dates anyone on the other side of the 405 freeway because it essentially becomes a long-distance relationship. It's only nine miles but the traffic is unbearable, especially on or around the 405.

On a later pandemic date, I met up with a music manager. I went to his house thinking this was just a date and I wasn't even going to hook up with him. But when I got there, he said, "I want you to meet somebody."

On our *first date*, this guy brings out his children. His *children*!

Let the fantasy begin! I was ready to be the best stepdad in the world to these little angels. I'd carry them on my shoulders while they ate cotton candy at the carnival. We'd have tough conversations about bullies at school. I'd read them bedtime stories, and they would wrap their little arms around me and tell me how much they love me. After the date, I never heard from that guy again. Oh, how I miss my little stepchildren.

Fuckboy Quiz

Through my extensive fuckboy dating history, I've named and categorized the fuckboys into a handy cheat sheet for the purpose of this book. If you're like me and have been through the fuckboy circus that is modern dating, you likely have a type or two. I invite you to take the quiz that follows to determine which fuckboy you're most attracted to so you can see what to watch out for in the future.

1. Where are you most likely to meet your fuckboy?
   a. At hot yoga or the juice bar
   b. At Weight Watchers, a shoe store, or sex shop
   c. At the coffee shop or bookstore
   d. At church or the country club
   e. On a dating app
   f. At a gala or event
   g. At the hospital or courthouse (any place where rescuing is involved)
   h. After he rear-ends you on the street
   i. At the bar after three shots of tequila

2. You make a connection with someone, what's the first thing they say to you?
   a. Your aura is breathtaking!

b. Your (insert body part) is so hot!

c. Hey, I think I got your matcha latte by mistake.

d. Wanna go somewhere and talk? My mom is watching.

e. I love your pictures, wanna FaceTime?

f. I don't usually do this, but would you like to come back to my place after the party?

g. Hey there, brought you an ice pack/coffee.

h. I'm not one to mince words. I think we could have a good time together. Let's get out of here.

i. Wanna do some blow with me in the bathroom?

3. Where do you go on your first date?

a. A sound bath followed by a colon cleanse

b. Fatburger or the local porn shop

c. Wherever's cool

d. His mother's house for dinner

e. A Zoom room with perfect lighting and angles

f. A celebrity party in the Hollywood Hills

g. The hospital or courthouse cafeteria

h. The back seat of his '91 Camry

i. Your place with him in your bathroom losing his battle with the cocaine shits

4. What happens at the end of the date?

a. He asks if he can stick a crystal up your ass.

b. He cries in shame because he knows his fetish made you feel weird. "I'm sorry, I don't know what's wrong with me," he sobs, as you comfort him.

c. You've already planned your wedding.

d. His mom tells you its past her son's bedtime so you should probably be going.

e. You both "finish" and leave the Zoom meeting.

f. After fucking in someone's bedroom at the party, you walk through a sea of former/current lovers, all glaring at you as you exit.

g. He grabs the check because you forgot your wallet, and you both grab each other in the parking lot.

h. With him saying, "Kick rocks, fuck buddy," as he hurries you out of his car and peels out of the parking lot.

i. With him stumbling out of your place at seven in the morning, your belongings hidden in his jacket.

5. How does the "situation-ship" usually end?

a. Your finding out he went to Tahiti for a silent retreat

b. You're five pounds heavier or you have retail therapied yourself into a new pair of Jimmy Choo's you can't afford.

c. Crying to your friends over your made-up relationship

d. With an angry voice mail from his mother and a pile of his unwashed laundry

e. With a high phone/Zoom bill and zero human touch

f. Blacklisted with blue balls

g. Sobbing in your therapist's office . . . again.

h. At the clinic with fucking chlamydia . . . again.

i. With an insurance claim and/or police report

Types of Fuckboys (results):

a. If you answered mostly a's, your fuckboy type is the **Spiritual Guru.**

b. If you answered mostly b's, you're into the **Fetishizer Fuckboy.**

c. If you answered mostly c's, your fuckboy type is
   Mr. No Strings Attached.
d. If you answered mostly d's, get ready to babysit your
   Man-Child Fuckboy.
e. If you answered mostly e's, you're on the screen with a
   Long-Distance Fuckboy.
f. If you answered mostly f's, you've got yourself a
   Celebrity Fuckboy.
g. If you answered mostly g's, your fuckboy is **Mr. Knight
   in Shining Armor.**
h. If you answered mostly h's, you've got an **Asshole
   Fuckboy** on your hands.
i. If you answered mostly i's, giddyup, you've lassoed
   yourself a **Cocaine Cowboy.**

Each of these fuckboy types are covered in more depth in chapter two in the Fuckboy Wall of Shame. Feel free to flip ahead and see what the Wall of Shame says about your fuckboy. Then come back for more on how to avoid these fuckboy pitfalls. Don't worry, we're all in this together.

FUCKBOY LESSON *Number One*

If they see you only as parts, whether in person or on a screen, you'll never be a whole human being to them.

The silver lining of my pandemic cloud was that I had space to do some real healing around body positivity and my struggles with an eating disorder. For the first time, I addressed my insecurities head-on and unpacked my shame around food and body size. Sure, it was traumatizing and lonely. But also, for the first time, I'd started to appreciate my body. I wasn't obsessing over every little thing I ate. If I wanted a cheese-burger, I knew I wasn't going to be seeing anyone, so I let myself enjoy a cheeseburger. Allowing myself those occasional indulgences stopped my cycle of deprivation and binging. All of that pressure I had willingly put on myself about my weight and my appearance began to fade. There were still many fuck-boys out there ready to waste my time.

But I had a moment of clarity: I didn't want superficial screen romance. I wanted love. Real self-love like the kind prophesied by Mary J. Blige, which I was just starting to expe-rience. And suddenly, my fuckboys were not a complete waste of time. They were an inspiration! My wild dating tales pro-vided me with valuable material that I can pass on to you in this book. Little did these fuckboys know I would one day be describing them, organizing and categorizing them, for my Fuckboy Wall of Shame.

CHAPTER TWO

The Kingdom of Fuckboys

Not only are fuckboys boring, but in my experience, there are only nine types of them. In this dark and not-so-mysterious kingdom, each type of fuckboy comes in different sizes, colors, and shapes, but they're all about the same things: sex, lies, and ghosting. Not to worry, lovely reader, I have sacrificed myself on the fuckboy altar to bring you the Fuckboy Wall of Shame so you can spot these problematic lover boys a mile away . . . and run in the other direction. If you find yourself attracted to a certain type of fuckboy, don't be hard on yourself. They've developed these personas because they know the personas work. But they don't have to work on you, anymore.

The Fuckboy Wall of Shame

Anyone who's done time in the modern dating world probably has their own trusty list of fuckboy archetypes. If you don't, not to worry, I got you covered. You can borrow my Fuckboy Wall of Shame and add a few of your own if you think I've missed some. These archetypes correspond with the Fuckboy Quiz from chapter one, so if you haven't taken the quiz, feel free to go back and do so now.

Spiritual guru fuckboy

I may seem enlightened but honestly, I'm just dying to use one of my energy healing crystals on you while you go down on me. You might find me hitting on you in the middle of hot yoga or as you're puking your guts out during an Ayahuasca trip. Anytime you try to hold me accountable, I'll claim you're just not spiritual enough for me or that we're not vibrating on the same frequency. Sure, I can be charismatic in public, but in private, I'll lock you into an hour of uncomfortable prolonged eye contact and then tell you after I get off that I don't reciprocate because I'm too spiritually "evolved."

Fetishizer fuckboy

You may be crying your eyes out at Overeaters Anonymous, but I'll be licking my lips as I imagine you jamming french fries in your mouth. At first, I'll seem obsessed with you when you catch me staring at a part of your body, like your stomach or your feet. The attention may feel good, until I'm begging you to stuff your face with donuts and burgers or do weird things to me with your feet. Later, I'll burst into tears because I feel weird about my fetish, making you comfort me for an hour after the weirdest sexual encounter of your life. Then I'll reject you because of my own shame.

No-strings-attached fuckboy

If you're looking to have sex with a cute, sweet guy with no strings attached, only to catch feelings and get your heart broken, then I am the fuckboy for you. I'm all about the meet cute at your local flower or coffee shop. Sure, it's just casual  sex. But I'll be so sweet, fun, and easy to be around, you won't be able to resist. What's the harm in fantasizing about a life together? It doesn't even have to be fantasies of the real me, you can just make stuff up. This should be easy since we'll only see each other at 3:00 a.m. after a night at the bars. I'm a total blank slate on which you can project all your relationship fantasies. But eventually I'll ghost you because of my own relationship phobias.

Man-child fuckboy

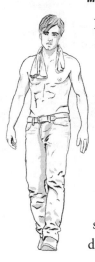

If you want to date not just me but also my overbearing mother, then get ready for the most awkward throuple ever. If you see me at church or the country club, rest assured, my helicopter mother has already seen you coming for miles. Sure, I'm nice, I have a good job and a supportive family. But you'll soon find out that my mother cooks all of my meals and comes over on weekends to clean my apartment and do my laundry. I don't know how to do any adult thing, such as committing to a long-term relationship or pay taxes. If you'd rather babysit than go on a date, I'm the man-child for you!

Long distance fuckboy

The pandemic did a number on all of us. But it especially hit me hard. I am now incapable of a close, in-person relationship and will string you along on video dates, texts, and phone calls forever. I've got all the best lighting and angles for the best video chat sex you've ever had, but you'll never see my whole body all at the same time. I'm great with words. In fact, I'm a real Casanova. But if you expect me to travel forty-five minutes to see you in person if you live on the other side of the 405, forget it. That's waaaaay too much to ask.

Celebrity fuckboy

If you want a well-connected guy who dangles the ever-elusive carrot of "helping you with your career" or "introducing you to Beyoncé," then I'm the fuckboy to fuck with. I've got a great smile and a trash personality. My ego is unchecked, which means you could find yourself at a party in a room with ten other people I'm fucking. I'll promise you the world. The problem is, I've already promised a dozen other lovers the same, and they all want to collect on that promise. If you like feeling shitty about yourself, come on in to the celebrity party.

Knight-in-shining-armor fuckboy

Here I come to save you from yourself! I'm
your knight-in-shining-armor fuckboy, and I'm
here with the tissues to dry your tears, honey. I
always happen to be in the right place at the
right time, when you are a total mess and I look
like a hero you've been waiting for. I'm what
you call a perfect rebound after a long, traumatic relationship. I've got it all, looks, sen-
sitivity, compassion, and I'm great in bed.
So what's the problem? You'll be so caught
up in your own suffering that you'll miss
all of my red flags. Sure, I'm not treating
you the way your ex did, but you'll catch me cheating in a year
because you didn't notice me checking out other people while you
were crying on my shoulder.

Asshole fuckboy

Maybe you're tired of dating nice guys (who pretend to
be friends with you but have a hidden agenda). If so, I'm
the bad boy for you. Just look for the chaos storm and
I'll be in the center of it. I don't waste my energy pretending to be a good guy. You know exactly what I'm
about. I'll flirt with other people right in front of
you, and it'll just make you want me even more. I'll
tell you I'm not the relationship type. "Me neither!"
you'll say as you fantasize about the house we'll buy
together after we get married. *I can change him. I'll be
the only one who can*, you'll think, ignoring the trail of

broken hearts in my wake. You'll gobble it up as I insult you to your face and say, "I'm just kidding! You're so sensitive." Then you'll act surprised when I have selfish sex with you and ghost you.

Cocaine cowboy fuckboy

Guess who just got outta rehab and is ready to tie one off! I'm the life of the party at the club, but when I go back to your place, I'll be trapped in your bathroom either puking or shitting. I'll fuck you and then steal your stuff as I stumble out your door at 7:00 a.m. Sure, I can be a lot of fun. But stay with me too long and you'll have to get a new social security number after I squat in your apartment for three months and steal your identity. I may not break your heart, but I'll fuck up your life if I get the chance. Stick to doing cocaine and fucking in the bathroom stall at the club with this guy right here and *never* tell him where you live.

Now, BEFORE YOU delete all your dating apps and smash your phone to pieces, I want you to know we've all been there. There is no shame in being tricked into a situation-ship with one of these fuck-boys. I call them situation-ships instead of relationships because nobody's "relating" in Fuckboy Land. It's also okay if you've been on both sides of the dating fence. No judgment here!

We've All Been a Fuckboy

Come on, admit it. Even if you don't identify as male, we've all been some type of fuckboy. As demonstrated on my Fuckboy Wall of Shame, they're not all necessarily assholes. Some of us have been the sweet fuckboy. I know I was. For a while, I was the guy who would go on a date with someone, maybe hook up with him, and then I'd end it and never talk to him again. Two or three dates were enough for me. I wasn't doing that to be an asshole; I was just in a phase where I didn't want to be in a serious relationship. Looking back on that, I'm sure I'm on someone else's Fuckboy Wall of Shame. Nobody gets out of modern dating unscathed. I've hurt people's feelings, you've hurt people's feelings, and we've all certainly had our feelings hurt.

Before my fuckboy phase, I had just gone through a serious breakup. If there was a burn unit for failed relationships, I would have been in the intensive care ward. My ex burned me bad. He cheated on me, lied to me, and broke my precious, already traumatized heart. I fell into a depression and decided to be single for about two years (more on that later). During that time, I didn't hook up with anybody. My self-worth was in the gutter, and I just couldn't imagine putting myself out there again, at least not in a serious way. I didn't think anyone would accept my body or love me for who I am. So I fasted from dating. I'd like to say I used that time to contemplate the reason I stayed in such unhealthy, tumultuous relationships and came out a whole new, wiser person. But instead, when I emerged from my cave of solitude, I was thirsty AF and ready to have some fun!

Was I intentionally and maliciously hurting people? No, not at all. Becoming a fuckboy was my shield, protecting me from being hurt by fuckboys. They couldn't hurt me if I did it to them first.

So I became the Well-Intended Fuckboy on somebody's Wall of Shame, probably many somebodies. I wasn't trying to lead people on by taking them on many dates and then ghosting, only to reappear once they were over me to hurt them again. No. We would have a good time and leave it at that. I like to believe I was the likable fuckboy . . . wasn't I? It may seem like a fuckboy is a fuckboy, but as someone who's experienced both, I'd take a Well-Intended Fuckboy over a malicious one, like-oh, I don't know, the Cocaine Cowboy perhaps?

The Cocaine Cowboy

I met him at a bar, and I'll be honest, I was pretty intoxicated. I was new to the gay dating scene and hadn't fooled around with many guys yet. Out of nowhere, this guy with a John Wayne swagger and a cowboy hat strutted up to the bar. Little did I know that swagger was the result of who knows how much blow he'd snorted before he got there. He was incredibly hot. He accompanied me to the bathroom where he snorted massive lines of cocaine on the back of the toilet and put a cigarette out in the palm of his hand. All I could think was, "Ooh, he's so rugged. That's sexy as hell!" I couldn't wait to get him back to my place.

My excitement quickly turned to disgust when, as soon as we got to my place, he hightailed it to my bathroom and proceeded to destroy my toilet with his cocaine shits. Well, at least he showered after he blew up my bathroom. When he came out, I was ready to have fun.

Unfortunately, our hookup was delayed again when he started crying to me about his dead brother. Of course, I cared and wanted him to let it out, but this was not the night I'd expected by a long shot. I was still new to dating men and was beginning to wonder if they were all like this. Later, I'd come to understand that while not all men are like this, all fuckboys definitely are, in one way or another. They shit on you, relieve themselves (either physically or emotionally), and then leave you unsatisfied or completely disgusted.

After his crying session, I didn't feel comfortable going down on him. So I decided to give him a hand job. There was only one problem, no lube. My eyes shifted to the self-tanner on the counter, then back to my tear-soaked date, the smell of his coke shits still lingering in the air. *He won't care*, I thought as I squirted a big dollop into my hand. He had a great time.

The odor wafting in the air the next morning let me know he wasn't quite done destroying my bathroom. I glanced over and saw him washing the self-tanner off his dick in my bathroom sink. *I wonder how long it will take me to get the tan stains out of the porcelain*, I thought. "Okay, buddy, you've gotta leave now," I said. I'd seen, heard, and smelled enough for one night. He stole my iPad on his way out.

An hour later, he called to tell me he was in love with me but that his husband wouldn't approve. I often wonder if his husband noticed that sun-kissed glow on his partner's bikini area.

Why We Love Fuckboys

In my opinion, one of the reasons we love fuckboys is because they represent something unattainable. If an unattainable guy is interested in us, it must mean we're worthy and special, right? Okay, maybe it was just me, but meeting a new fuckboy was like a drug. I got high on the validation, intoxicated by the thrill of those initial sparks flying between the fuckboy-of-the-moment and me. I knew it would only lead to pain, embarrassment, and heartache, yet it still pulled at me. If I'm honest, it still does. But just like a recovered addict, I now have the tools to keep myself from "using" again.

As I sit here writing this chapter, my partner and I have been together for a little over two years. We're happily in love. But during our first few months of dating, I was still thinking about a fuckboy I'd been with before. Like so many others, this guy was clearly a dead end. So what the fuck was I doing obsessing over him when I had a perfectly wonderful partner right in front of me? My partner loves me and takes care of me. But I was still detoxing from the validation and the oh-so-exhilarating chaos chemicals that surged through my body when a hot stranger noticed me from across the room. I'd put them up on a fuckboy pedestal and let the fantasies fly until the room was spinning. But none of that can compare to looking beside me and seeing a stable human being who genuinely cares about me, who wants to see me succeed, who shares my joy and my grief . . . someone who loves me unconditionally.

If you haven't found your Waldo yet, don't worry. I can help you turn down the fuckboy noise so you can find the real ones. Once you understand the warning signs, you'll be able to tune your fuckboy detector to pick up even the slightest of red flags.

Fuckboy Warning Signs

As a gay man in fuckboy central, a.k.a. West Hollywood, it can be tricky to discern whether the cute guy in front of you is genuinely looking for a relationship or leading you down the well-worn fuckboy path. Fortunately, they leave little clues everywhere they go that, to the keen eye, are strong early indicators that you're entering fuckboy territory.

Common types of fuckboy behaviors

1. **Aloof AF Andy**—If you're on a date with a fuckboy and he is constantly looking over your shoulder to see who else is in the room, you may want to get the fuck out of said room.

2. **Rushy Rusherpants**—If you've only been on a few dates with someone and they tell you they want to move in together, hang up and call your therapist. Moving too fast is a huge red flag. If they're not willing to allow the relationship to unfold naturally, they're either dysregulated and don't understand basic laws of time and connection, or they're hiding something and want to ensnare you before you find out so it's harder for you to leave.

3. **Donnie Dumper**—If you've just met this person and they're sobbing over their dead brother after blowing up your bathroom, chances are you're just a receptacle for not only cum but all of their unprocessed emotions. Find the nearest exit while you can!

4. **Hidey-Hole Harry**—This guy may want to meet you for a date in a different town or only at your place. Hot tip, he's doing that because he's either married or in a relationship and doesn't want to be recognized when he's out with you. Tell his spouse they can have him and take yourself to dinner instead.

5. **Love Bomber Larry**—You've known him for all of three hours, but Larry wants you to know that he's already madly in love with you. He'll blow up your phone after your first date with texts like, "I've never met anyone like you before. OMG you're amazing!" Then you'll never hear from him again.

I Just Can't Quit You

When I missed all the warning signs, I was easily tricked into believing that situation-ships had a chance past the first few encounters. Long after the moment was dead, I would be there, defibrillator in hand, desperate to reignite those intoxicating sparks from the first time we met. A hopeless Dr. Frankenstein, but with better hair. I'd sell my dignity for that rush of chaos and uncertainty, calling them when I knew they weren't interested or agreeing to see them again when I felt totally creeped out by their behavior. It wasn't so much that I missed the warning signs . . . you'd have to be blind, deaf, and unable to smell Mr. Cocaine Cowboy's red flags. It was that I was willing to overlook them because I had no self-worth and was desperate to be loved.

There's a psychological reason some of us are drawn to fuckboys. Psychotherapist Ashika Jain agrees with Pia Mellody that it's about our attachment style. Jain asserts that when we have parents who were emotionally unavailable or who abandoned us, we will subconsciously seek out that same type of attachment in our adult relationships. Those of us who grew up chasing love from distant caregivers tend to recreate that same dynamic later in life. We find comfort in what's familiar, even if it's not what's best for us. Some of us became fuckboys to get a taste of what it's like to hold the power of being love avoidant, like I did for a while. Even though I wouldn't consider myself a malicious fuckboy, I swung on both sides. Sometimes I was love addicted, and sometimes I was love avoidant.

Whenever I met someone new, I was certain their love would solve all my problems. But when the temporary buzz wore off, I'd be alone again, hands stained by self-tanner and the stench of shame. Pia Mellody asserts in her book *Facing Love Addiction: Giving Yourself the Power to Change the Way You Love*, there are two fears gripping the love addict:

1. The fear of abandonment
2. The fear of intimacy

The irony is that by pursuing that high of initial attraction, I was sacrificing the possibility of true connection with someone who was ready to love me the way I deserved. Some of this stems from childhood. I was abandoned by my dad and bullied relentlessly (I'll go further into this in chapter four), and I longed for someone to make me feel good about myself. Later, I learned that nobody else can make me feel good about myself. That validation I was seeking needed to come from within before I would ever attract external validation and a love that values me for who I am.

Finding internal validation has been a lifelong process for me. While I go into each of the ways I found love, respect, and validation for myself throughout this book, it was a long, hard road full of obstacles and setbacks. But at the core of all of the ways I've found internal validation is a compassionate curiosity about myself. Once I was able to ask myself questions without judgment, and receive the answers with compassion, I was able to see all the ways I'd learned to seek validation outside myself. For instance, when I examined the reason I loved chasing love-avoidant fuckboys, I found a deep loneliness that began with my father's absence, which I carried into adulthood. Despite what all the positive-thinking, self-love, self-care influencers say, it's not about flipping a magic switch that makes you suddenly adore and admire yourself. It takes the work of untangling all of the things wrapped around your self-esteem, examining them so they don't get reattached in a different form, and replacing those things with self-trust, compassion, respect, and a healthy relationship with yourself, so you can stop being your own worst fuckboy.

Fuckboy Harm Reduction

If you're reading this book and thinking, "But Ryan, I don't want a relationship. But I'm not a dick, either. I just want to have fun for a while without the demands and expectations of a relationship." My darling, I hear you! I was there once myself. Wanting to engage in casual sex doesn't make you a bad fuckboy. You can consciously choose to be a good fuckboy. Consider it fuckboy harm reduction. You can have all the fun you want, but as they say in liquor ads, please enjoy responsibly.

Not all fuckboys are trash. Some of them really are just looking for fun without the complications of a relationship. Some know they're at a stage in their lives where they wouldn't make a good partner, but they still like to be touched. The good fuckboys become a problem when we lie to ourselves and fantasize about fixing them, changing them, or convincing them to be in a relationship with us when they've made it clear they don't want one. If a fuckboy tells you he doesn't want anything serious, believe him. And if you know you tend to get attached, stay away from the good fuckboys (as well as the bad ones).

Deconstructing the Fuckboy

Make a list of the fuckboys you've dated and categorize them for your own Fuckboy Wall of Shame. Do you notice any patterns? Once you have them categorized, ask yourself the following:

- Which fuckboy category am I drawn to the most?

- What need am I trying to fulfill with this fuckboy category?

- How can I fulfill that need for myself instead of relying on the fuckboy?

ARE YOU A GOOD FUCKBOY? OR A BAD FUCKBOY?

(in the voice of Glinda the Good Witch of
the North from *The Wizard of Oz*)

Good Fuckboys	Bad Fuckboys
• Tell you up front what to expect. For instance, "I'm not looking for a relationship."	• Will lead you on, love bomb you, and exploit your hopes that this will turn into a relationship.
• Don't tell you they'll call when they don't plan on calling you again.	• Tell you they'll call you, but you never hear from them again.
• Don't make plans for the future if they don't plan on seeing you again.	• Promise you the moon but never deliver. They owe the moon to a lot of frustrated lovers.
• Take responsibility for their own emotional needs.	• Make you wipe their tears and be a vessel for their shame before ghosting you.
• Don't insult your intelligence. They set your expectations instead of leading you on.	• Lie right to your face until you find out they're married, an addict, or an ex-con.
• Are looking for a good time, no strings attached.	• Are looking for someone they can use and then discard.
• Treat you like a human being, not an object.	• Treat you like a toy or an object.
• End things respectfully instead of ghosting.	• Ghost you as soon as they get bored or feel embarrassed about their shitty behavior.
• Show up when you make plans.	• Cancel plans last minute.

FUCKBOY LESSON *Number Two*

If you're going to be a fuckboy, at least try to be a good fuckboy so you don't end up on someone's Wall of Shame.

EXITING THE KINGDOM OF FUCKBOYS

In this twisted kingdom, there are no princes or princesses. The only knights in shining armor are the ones who want to give you a quick stabby, stabby with their big hard sword before ditching you for the stable boy. The fairy tales in this land never lead to a "happily ever after" ending (even if there is a happy ending). All the tales of this land end with cocaine shits, self-tanned dicks, and a stolen iPad. Handsome guys transform into toads before your very eyes. If there's a glass slipper, it's getting jammed in your asshole when you least expect it. The only heroes are the ones who pack up their gowns and flee the Kingdom of Fuckboys before the clock strikes midnight and they turn into a pumpkin. Still thinking of turning back? Let's unpack our addiction to dicks in chapter three.

CHAPTER THREE

Addicted to Dick (and Assholes)

At first the change was subtle, she put $500 on red when I knew she didn't like gambling and was usually cautious with her money. She was losing control of her emotions over the smallest things. It was my thirtieth birthday, just before Valentine's Day. My best friend, Lizzie, and I celebrated in Vegas on a long weekend getaway. But as the weekend unfolded, I could tell something was . . . off about Lizzie. I offered to cancel my flight so I could drive her home. She refused. So I got on a plane to head back to Los Angeles with the nagging thought like a tack hammer in the back of my mind that she shouldn't be alone. As I sat in my seat on the airplane, just before takeoff, my phone rang. It was the hotel where we'd been staying.

"Hi, uh . . . your guest is having a problem. She's screaming, getting aggressive with our staff, and causing a scene. Are you able to come and get her?"

My heart sank. I knew I shouldn't have left her. In an instant, I was off the plane and back at the Vegas hotel, where I could see that Lizzie was in dire need of mental health care. I convinced her to come with me to the hospital so we could get her examined. The whole way to the hospital, she insisted she was fine. "I don't know what you're talking about." It was clear that she was not fine.

The doctors glanced at Lizzie, who I'd known for fifteen years at the time, and diagnosed her as having alcohol withdrawal symptoms. I'm sure Las Vegas doctors see that kind of thing all the time. But I knew they were missing the problem, so I pulled the doctor aside and told him I thought she was having a psychotic break. The doctor didn't believe me, so I reluctantly booked us on a flight home to Los Angeles. I invited her back to my place to spend the night as I was terrified to let her sleep alone. In the middle of the night and to my horror, my best friend began singing opera and talking to the walls. She came running out of the bedroom to tell me she had a vision that I was going to be killed in a car accident. I drove her to UCLA Medical Center, hoping to get a better response from the doctors there. They diagnosed her with a panic disorder and admitted her for the night.

I was seeing a Canadian guy at the time, and we'd made plans that night, the same night a tragedy changed my best friend forever. I texted the Canadian explaining what happened and that I was going to be late. We had originally planned to meet at 7:30 p.m. He was cooking dinner for us for Valentine's Day. I left at around 9:00, shortly after they admitted Lizzie to the hospital. Sure, I was an hour and a half late, but I had a valid reason, and I'd let him know it was an emergency.

Later, we would find out Lizzie had an inoperable brain tumor that had completely changed her personality. She was never the same again. That night was horrible and traumatic, and I refused to leave her side until she was safe, dinner plans be damned.

In the car, on the way to his place, I was still processing the trauma of what had happened. My phone lit up with a text from this Canadian fuckboy saying, "You might want to order pizza."

Confused, I responded, "Why?"

"Because the food I made got cold and I threw it out."

What?

If I'd had any self-respect, I would have turned around and gone home. But did I do that? Nope! My deep gutter self-esteem and I hung our heads, ordered pizza, and brought our Canadian boy his Valentine's Day gift.

"Oh, I actually ate your gift," he shrugged. "So, you know, I don't have it."

My mind flashed to two weeks earlier. It was my birthday, and he said he didn't get me anything because he was going to get me a really nice Valentine's Day gift. I burst into tears in front of him, crying out all the pain from the last twenty-four hours. In a puddle of trauma, devastation, and shame, I finally excused myself and left.

The worst part of the date (though certainly not the night)? I wasn't even attracted to this guy. I knew he was a total asshole, but I was so upside down from my last relationship, I had no idea if my feelings were valid. I was awash in heartbreak and hunger . . . not just for the dinner he'd thrown out but for someone to comfort and love me in one of my darkest moments.

The moral of the story is this: if you think you're being treated poorly by a total dick, you're probably being treated poorly by a total dick. Sure, that bad boy vibe can be so addictive. They have this way of making us feel important and wanted. One minute. But the next minute, you're crying on his doorstep because he ate all of your Valentine chocolates and dumped your dinner in the trash. For me, it was an intoxicating roller-coaster ride, and I was firmly buckled in.

Maybe because I was so unstable the scream-inducing drops and sharp unpredictable turns felt . . . normal.

He had bad breath anyway. Lizzie told him so to his face at a get-together a few weeks later. "Your breath smells like a decaying body," she said plainly. Her tumor had left her without a filter, and she had no problem telling it like it is. He broke up with me that night.

It was only a three-month whirlwind romance, but it took my self-esteem from the gutter all the way to the bottom of the Pacific. I still find myself wondering, how could a guy I wasn't even into break my heart? My friends didn't like him; I didn't like him. But because I was on the heels of a four-year relationship that dragged me through the depths of borderline personality disorder and gaslighting hell, I was willing to settle for anyone who didn't make me question my own reality.

What is my problem? I asked myself this question on more than one occasion. Why is it that when I'm at my lowest, I always go for the Asshole Fuckboy, a.k.a. The Dick.

Fire Starters

Even after Lizzie had insulted my Canadian fuckboy and he broke up with me via text, I still wanted him . . . after all of that. Obviously, our relationship was doomed from the start, so even my desperate need for his attention couldn't hold the severed ends of our casual flings together. He did reach out to me about a year later. They always reach back out because they're fire starters. After they've set every other possible relationship ablaze, they always come knocking. I mean there are only so many gay men in West Hollywood, and he'd probably burned through all of them . . . twice.

So what is it about the Asshole Fuckboy that makes us betray and abandon ourselves? Part of it may have to do with the sense of danger and excitement swirling around every encounter with them. For me, it felt like a departure from everyday life. Some of us get bored with the nice ones. Some of us (it's me, I'm "us") equate a guy's shitty personality with excitement, a thrill that makes our hearts pump and our pupils widen, even if we know we're in for a huge crash. Will they call or won't they? The game of it all can be highly addictive and intoxicating. But in my experience, the negatives always outweigh those short bursts of chemicals coursing through our bodies. Eventually, if we don't want to destroy ourselves, we've got to stop fucking with assholes, no matter how good it feels temporarily.

For the Canadian fuckboy, I was clearly his back-burner bitch. He made me sleep on his couch when I came over, for fuck's sake. He called me when nobody else wanted him because he had burned all of his bridges. But he knew that I'd always be there, simmering on that back burner until he was ready to move me to the front for a few hours before shoving me to the back again. I used to think I was special when he called me again. But guys like him call everybody back. They recycle and reuse until they've thoroughly fucked everybody over. It's the fuckboy cycle of fuckery. And it never really ends.

Don't Be a Back-Burner Bitch—A Quick Guide

It's time to get off that back burner, babe. You want front-burner energy.

Signs you are being put on the back burner

- Their patterns change (that is, they usually text you every night and they suddenly stop).
- They don't commit to making plans with you.

- They won't introduce you to their friends.

- They say things like, "Let's just go with the flow" (see Fuckboy Decoder on page 54).

- If you feel in your gut something's off, something's probably off. Trust your gut.

How to avoid being back-burnered

- Say no the very first time they try to move you to the back burner.

- Pay attention to how they treat you and keep paying attention.

- Get off the roller coaster. If they are obsessed with you one minute and then disappear for days at a time, they're roping you into an addictive cycle of love bombing, followed by abuse or abandonment. Break the cycle. If they ignore you for three days and then try to call, don't rush to pick up. After three days, you will be at the end of your love-chemical brain detox and desperate for another hit, and they know it. Allow your brain more time to recalibrate back to normal levels of dopamine, serotonin, and oxytocin. Put yourself in love rehab.

- Hold them accountable. If they tell you they've thrown away your food after the worst night of your life and that you should order pizza, tell them you find that unacceptable and hurtful. Don't shield them from the pain they're causing. Turn your ass around and go home. If you stay after they pull a dick move like that, they'll know they can get away with doing it again and again and again.

- Once a ghost, always a ghost. Know that if they broke up with you or ghosted you before, they will do it again. So if they call you again in a year or two hoping you've forgotten what a jerk they are, don't fall for it. Write it down in a fuckboy journal if you have to so you can go back and read all the reasons not to take their call.

Before the Assholes, There Were the Bullies

As an overweight kid, riddled with acne, growing up in Baltimore, I suffered an excruciating amount of bullying. I was excluded, called horrible names, and became the target of many cruel pranks. Someone once put Super Glue in my hair. I was called "faggot" more times than I can count. One kid even got expelled because he hurled the slur at me so often. I ate lunch in the bathroom every day, and my life was a nightmare.

The final straw was the day I was giving a presentation in front of the class and a kid threw a pencil at me. Desperate for backup, I looked over and saw the teacher . . . laughing. These kids were torturing me daily, and not only did the teachers neglect their duty to protect me, but that laughter gave students the green light to keep bullying me. That day, I went home and told my mom I couldn't take it anymore and that I was going to kill myself if I had to go back to school. Thankfully, she took my cry for help seriously and let me homeschool, or I might not be here today.

When I left the school, all that pain didn't just disappear. I was consumed by a deep depression that eventually turned into anger. I wanted to get even. I wanted the power to make someone else feel inferior. While I never became a full-fledged bully, I did start pushing back when I was attacked, probably more forcefully than necessary. Later, that desire to have power when I felt so powerless translated into becoming a fuckboy myself. I would be the one calling the shots, the one to ghost a guy first before they could do it to me. When I think about how desperate I was to have a sense of control over my life, I can't help but wonder if that's a common feeling among other fuckboys too.

I went on to judge others as I had once been judged. I was never mean about it. But I'm ashamed to say that I didn't date anyone who weighed more than I did. I only liked someone if other people thought they were good-looking. It's difficult to admit, but dating an attractive person gave me credibility. I hid under the false confidence that, if I was with someone who was gorgeous, that meant I must be gorgeous by association. Deep down, I believed that people who mistreated me were better than me.

The truth is, the first time I rejected someone, I felt empowered, but I also felt guilty because I knew what it was like to be on the receiving end of that rejection. For far too long, I went out with people in whom I had zero interest because I liked the attention. To make matters worse, turning people down made me feel more attractive. To be clear, I wasn't turning people down for the hell of it. But the boost was still there. This false sense of confidence overpowered any lingering feelings of guilt I had. Eventually I started to wonder, why did excluding or rejecting someone give me a confidence boost (however superficial)? Of course, I didn't have to accept every date that was presented to me. But the rejection should've been more selective and based on things like self-respect (not just whether my friends thought they were hot). Instead, my broken method of selection landed me with a creature of a fuckboy.

The Creature of the Night

On a hot summer night in Los Angeles, I was at a bar with friends when I met a total chaos tornado with rippling muscles and a nice smile. He gave me his number and told me to call him. My friends encouraged me to go have some fun with him. *Why not?* I thought. So I met him at this fancy spot in West Hollywood.

Later, we went back to his place for a drink, so he said. But he had other intentions. The night was going well, until I started going down on him. I was totally caught off guard when my date let out this high-pitched shriek that sounded like some prehistoric creature (hence the name, Creature of the Night). It completely threw me off. I left my body and could see myself like Samantha from *Sex and the City* sitting there looking at her watch while her date came. *Can we be done already? I'm so over this.*

I wish that were the end of the story.

After my screeching-pterodactyl date finished, I fell off his bed, slamming my rib cage hard on the edge of the nightstand. He was begging me to stay, but I'd had all I could take of this experience, stealing a bottle of liquor as I walked out the door. Before you judge, he promised me we were just going back to his place to have a drink, no sex. Then he pushed me to go down on him once we got there. I'd earned that drink (more than I realized at the time).

Two days later, I still had this sharp pain in my ribs, so I decided to have it checked out. I told the urgent care doctor about the pain in my ribs, and since I was already there, I mentioned that I had a sore throat and possibly pink eye. He took an X-ray and ran some tests. I left that day with a diagnosis of a cracked rib . . . and chlamydia.

When I told Creature of the Night that he'd given me chlamydia, he responded with "Did I?"

"Yeah, you asshole," I wrote back.

As if that wasn't bad enough, it turns out he was also living with his boyfriend, who just happened to be out of town during our shrieking Gollum hookup session. He hit me up for years, every time his boyfriend was out of town, telling me that he never stopped thinking about me.

You'd think I would have learned my lesson and said, "No, thank you." But I hooked up with him again. Thankfully, we were both STD free. It was one of the worst hookups ever. Same screeching, same dissatisfaction on my end. But I didn't completely mind. He was like my "Good Luck Chuck." Every time we saw each other, I wound up in a relationship with someone else right after him, and a fresh bottle of pilfered liquor. I considered it my chlamydia tax.

Who's the Real Bully?

It's not uncommon to assume the role of the bullies from our childhoods, in one sense or another. We take the baton in the relay race of abuse and carry it deep into ourselves, beating ourselves up with it. We hate ourselves long after the bully that hated us is gone. Sometimes, the self-hatred is so unbearable, we unload it on someone else. But it always comes back to us in one way or another until we deal with it. In the Creature of the Night situation, I was both the bully and the bullied. I knew I was going to make fun of this guy later to my friends. And he may or may not have known he had chlamydia. He certainly knew he wasn't planning on serving me drinks at his place, only dick.

When I entered my twenties, I had a firm grasp on that bully baton. I bullied myself into believing that if only I could lose weight, someone would love me. And at times, I did lose the weight, but I wasn't any happier. In fact, I wasn't me. I don't entirely embrace the body positivity space, but I do believe that we need to be who we are—emancipated from society's preconceived notions around beauty, looks, and body type. I didn't love myself, so I didn't honor myself in dating situations. I'd let big muscular guys like the Creature of the Night manipulate me into sex, even when I had zero interest. It was as if the physical injury and illness I acquired that night were direct representations of what I was doing to myself on the inside.

There's a saying, "Nothing changes if nothing changes." My self-worth wasn't changing, so my dating life wasn't changing. The same thing kept happening. I would either end up rejected and alone at the end of the night or I would be driving home with sore ribs, a stolen bottle of liquor, and an STD. My dating life had become my worst nightmare.

This vicious cycle was keeping me from love—but not just for others, because what I realized is prioritizing physical attraction above all else was actually my most lethal weapon of self-hatred. And I cut myself on it time and time again. The sad part was, as a new member of gay culture, and a former member of the straight world, I saw how everyone else around me was doing it too. They were sacrificing opportunities to have healthy, supportive, wonderful relationships for a match that went out as soon as it was lit.

This addiction to assholes keeps us from not only finding true love with others but from finding true love with ourselves. It's one of the ways we bully ourselves, by not only keeping us from the love we deserve but isolating us from communities of people who want to be in supportive and loving friendships and relationships. So how do we avoid the dick traps that fuckboys set for us in the dating world? One way is to understand what they really mean when they're running their game. Don't worry, I've made you a decoder to make sure you understand what your fuckboy is really trying to say.

Fuckboy Decoder

Coming to you live from the Red Flag Parade, we've got a list of the most common phrases I've heard from fuckboys, and what they really mean when they say these things.

- I've never met anyone like you before.
  - "Call me Casper because I'm going to ghost you faster than you can say 'boo.'"
- "You remind me of my ex."
  - I'm not over my ex and you'll never measure up to them.
- "I've never felt this connection before."
  - I am desperate for love.

"You have everything I'm looking for."
  - I have no clue what the fuck I'm looking for, but chances are, you ain't it.
- "I'm just going with the flow for now."
  - I have no intention of making you a priority.
- "I'm looking for that special someone."
  - I want you to think that someone special is you when I know it's not and will breadcrumb you along until you give me what I want.
- "I can't wait to see you again." (Immediately after a date)
  - You will never hear from me again.
- "You're so kind."
  - I know I can do whatever I want to you, and you'll keep coming back so I can break you again and again without remorse or accountability.

Dick-claimer: These translations are based on my personal experiences. I'm generalizing for educational and entertainment purposes. But to be fair, I've heard these phrases a lot, and they pretty much pan out the same way every time. I'm like a fuckboy scientist. I've done thorough research in the field.

In my pseudoscientific opinion, if you hear phrases like the ones mentioned previously, you're in Red Flag City. It usually takes about three months of dating exclusively for you to truly get to know someone. So it's crucial to pay attention during those first three months for red flags. And it's even more important to pay attention after, when their guards are coming down and they are revealing their true colors. Then, if they show themselves to be fuckboys, it's easier to detach.

Create Your Own Fuckboy Decoder

- Are you dating someone who says certain things consistently right before they let you down?

- Write down the common phrases you've heard from fuckboys.

- Now decode those phrases to illustrate what they actually mean.

- Compare notes with your friends over drinks. You can help each other decode!

FUCKBOY LESSON *Number Three*

Never take a fuckboy at face value (no matter how gorgeous that face is). Pay attention to what they do over what they say.

All the entertaining education in the world won't help us if we don't address the inner struggle that keeps us going back for assholes. At a certain point, we come to a fork in the road. One path leads to more chaotic messy dating scenarios, the other to a road less traveled, one that leads us to honest, vulnerable love for ourselves and others. But sometimes, before we can go forward, we have to understand where we've been. For many of us who grew accustomed to bullies in childhood, we may miss the warning signs in adulthood. If we miss the warning signs, we are likely to be blindsided by a jerk who throws away your birthday dinner and eats your Valentine's Day present.

Truth be told, there were warning signs before the Canadian fuckboy broke my heart on one of the worst nights of my life. But since I was used to obvious cruelty from the bullies in my childhood, I overlooked the more subtle warning signs. A good barometer for noticing shitty behavior is to think about someone you love and ask yourself: if someone I loved was being treated this way, would I find it acceptable? If the answer is no, it's probably time to reevaluate that situation-ship.

If you tend to go for the assholes, don't be too hard on yourself. We are often taught what to tolerate in childhood. If we had parents who were abusive, neglectful, hard on us, or prone to passive-aggressive behavior, our childhood brains calibrate our view of relationships accordingly. It can take a lifetime to learn to ask for better in our adult relationships. But once we see that it's possible to be treated with the love and respect we deserve, it becomes much harder to go back.

CHAPTER FOUR

Just Stop Fucking Yourself

He was the first fuckboy ever to ghost me, the OG (Original Ghoster). Before I'd ever laid eyes on this man, he was out the door . . . because I was still in the womb when he left. On the day I was born, I emerged from my mother's warm loving body and plunged immediately into a cold sterile void where my father's love should have been. As a drug addict who was having an affair with his coworker, he didn't have much space in his life for family. My parents divorced when I was six months old. After that, my relationship with the OG was a relentless cycle of abandonment and abuse, and it pressed deep grooves in my young brain until I believed this kind of relationship was "normal." Eventually, I subconsciously calibrated all of my future relationships to match these familiar patterns.

As a ghosted child, I harbored the belief that I was worthless. When you're a child of abuse, your heart speaks a different language than your mind. You don't have a connection to logic, and you justify the abuse, telling your heart it's not broken so you can survive. I carried that feeling of worthlessness into the world with me, through every relationship, every job, every important decision. It clouded all aspects of my life.

For years, I clung to the fantasy that the OG wasn't my real dad. I obsessed over this idea, often pleading with my mom, "Look, mom, you can tell me if you had an affair. Come on, just tell me he's not my real dad." I was certain that somewhere out there was a man who adored me and wanted desperately to be with me. This was the start of my tendency toward emotional masturbation. I'd fantasize about someone who didn't exist, my *real* dad, a hero who would arrive any minute to rescue me and teach me how to be a man of honor, to help me deal with the pain of the OG's absence. This coping mechanism kept hope alive as I teetered along a cliff's edge overlooking a deep chasm of despair. It helped me survive. If the OG was my real dad, that meant I was unlovable, not worth getting clean for and showing up at my birthday parties, not important enough for even a phone call. My childhood brain just couldn't hold the pain of those thoughts.

My dad ghosted me so much, I started making him pay to talk to me. I'd charge him fifty dollars per week to talk to me when I became an adult. It was my way of getting back at him for the time he was incarcerated for not paying child support. But it made my future relationships with men transactional, fifty dollars here, a stolen bottle of liquor there, a fleeting sense of validation, a hot guy on my phone making me feel important. All of it began from that teenage place of feeling like I never got what I needed from the OG. I replaced love with money, food, and a fleeting sense of power from finally being the one in control when my dad finally wanted to talk to me.

My father's abuse and neglect, in addition to the bullying at school, made me feel powerless as a kid. While I was angry at those bullies, my belly burned with rage at my father. *Maybe if my dad was around and showed me how to hit a fucking baseball I wouldn't be called a fag all the time*, I thought. I didn't have a male role model to teach me how to stand up for myself. I needed a knight in shining armor, a strong man to show me what to do when a twelve-year-old little shit spews hatred at you in the school halls. My mother was amazing, but without the love, belonging, and validation from a father figure, I felt an unbearable ache of loneliness. That ache was so profound, I didn't care what I had to do, or how much I had to hurt myself, to ease the pain. At thirteen years old, I developed an eating disorder that I would go on to battle for two decades. If only I'd known that my dad ghosting me had very little to do with me, and everything to do with him.

Why Do People Ghost?

When I was choosing unavailable men and getting ghosted all the time, it was baffling to me. You can suck my dick and be inside me but have a problem calling or texting me to say it's not working out? While examining my old tendency to pick dates who allowed me to relive my abuse and abandonment issues, I realized something. These acts of ghosting had very little to do with me. But my habit of pursuing men who were destined to abandon me was a pattern I chose and accepted willingly. It was time for me to learn healthy relationship behaviors that were never modeled for me in childhood. Even a basic understanding of how to end a relationship would save me a world of pain.

As someone who has been ghosted, and done a bit of ghosting myself, I've gained some valuable insights as to why people ghost.

Spoiler, it rarely has anything to do with the person being ghosted. It's probably not your fault, and honestly, they likely did you a favor since people who ghost are rarely ready for a healthy relationship. Still, if it's keeping you awake at night, wondering why you've been ghosted, a list of reasons might set your mind at ease.

Reasons people ghost

- Fear of intimacy
- Insecurity
- Fear of telling the truth/facing the truth about themselves
- Embarrassment about their bad behavior
- Too immature to have a grown-up conversation that ends things respectfully
- Can't deal with the thought of hurting someone (which usually signals unresolved childhood trauma and not being able to deal with difficult emotions)
- Fear of conflict/confrontation (see above regarding unresolved childhood trauma)
- Lack of courage
- Fear of growing up
- A sociopathic lack of basic empathy

The truth is none of us make it out of this life unscathed. So many of us in the dating world are just playing out the familiar relationship patterns we experienced in childhood. As your friendly guide and former mayor of the ghost town of dysfunctional situation-ships, I understand the struggle. If you're dating in this modern Tinder-box of trauma where every swipe potentially strikes a "match," you've likely been ghosted once or twice.

When I got ghosted, I thought it was all about me. I would obsess over whether they thought I was too fat, if I said something wrong, or if I just wasn't lovable enough. I never considered that I was dealing with complicated people (just like me) with their own pasts that they'd learned to survive using defense mechanisms, such as ghosting. I wish I could go back to talk to my past self, when I was so disturbed at being ghosted, and say, "It's not your fault and has very little to do with you." To think of all of the suffering from taking things personally I could have avoided when it wasn't about me at all.

I try to live without regret as much as possible. Without these stories, I wouldn't be writing this book. But even though I don't regret the past, I do appreciate the freedom that comes with learning from my mistakes. Sure, I allowed ghosting to put me in a cage of shame and despair, but I didn't stay there. I picked the lock and came out with notes for everyone else. Yes, I was obsessing about the guys who'd ghosted me, but I was also doing my research. That is when I learned that ghosting can be nuanced. If you're not careful, it can be difficult to detect because it is sometimes disguised as something else. While I understand and have compassion for people who ghost, I don't have to fall for it ever again. And I can teach others how to spot the various types of ghosting, so you don't fall for it either.

As it turns out, there are more ways than one to ghost a person. Believe me, I've experienced them all, from both sides.

Types of Ghosting

Here are the different ways of abandoning someone in the dating world, paraphrased from Nate Swanner's The Manual.

- **Ghosting**—make like a ghost and vanish without a trace. This term is used for anyone who has dropped off the face of the earth, suddenly stops talking to you, won't take your calls, won't respond to your texts, blocks you on social media, and becomes the ghost of fuckboy past. It's a thing people do when they don't have the courage to break up with someone in a dignified way. Or they got what they wanted and have no further interest in pursuing a relationship. This leaves the ghostee feeling confused, hurt, and angry . . . not that the ghoster would notice.

- **Haunting**—after ghosting you and disappearing for a significant amount of time, the haunter will stealth-stalk your social media, maybe liking one of your posts or sending an emoji reaction to one of your stories. This low-effort engagement is like low self-esteem bait. If you take it, they'll know you don't have enough respect for yourself to ignore or block them. They'll view your eagerness as low hanging fruit, which they'll pluck, take one bite of, and toss back in the dating pool before ghosting you again. It's best to board up this ghost back in his little haunted house.

- **Submarining**—rather than the half-hearted, more subtle approach of a haunter, this fuckboy will suddenly pop back up in your life like a submarine resurfacing out of the water. It's always when you least expect it and usually when you've just gotten over them. The submariner is eager to rekindle the flame, most likely because they've already tainted all the dating waters, and nobody wants anything to do with them. They may use the passage of time to shield them from the accountability of their behavior in the past, hoping you will have forgotten about it. They'll act like nothing happened and try to lure you into another situation-ship, only to slink back into the dark waters of the oblivion until next time. When that submarine pops up, it's best to push it right back down and keep moving.

- **Zombieing**—the zombie will hobble back to you, sometimes years after they vanished, wounded and contrite, hoping to resurrect a dead connection. This zombie may mumble some insincere apologies or make false promises and insist they've changed. But if you pay attention, you can smell the decaying flesh of their old betrayals as if it were rotting off their bones in front of you. Let that putrid stench remind you not to make this grave mistake again.

- **Orbiting**—this one's for the sneaky little phantoms. They'll ghost you, then creep on your social media pages to find out what you're up to. They may be curious, or they may be looking for a reason to pop back into your life, like when they see that you're happy and fulfilled and they want to steal that joy or status for themselves. While you're doing your best to move on, they'll lurk in your orbit, ready to strike when the moment is right. If you're worried they might enter your atmosphere again, the block button is a great way to eject them from your life so they can't stealth-stalk you.

- **Breadcrumbing**—just like Hansel and Gretel, the kids in the German fable that dropped breadcrumbs in the woods so they could find their way home, a breadcrumber will drop a trail of tiny "love" morsels so you'll follow them into the fuckboy woods. They may drop subtle hints to your friends that they're in town and want to see you again. Or they'll send you a small text here, a social media comment there, until you're gobbling up those crumbs and skipping gleefully right into the witch's hut to be cooked in the oven of loneliness. Hot tip: if they're stringing you along, they don't like you; they like the attention they're getting from you. As soon as they get more favorable attention from someone else, they'll drop you like the witch dropped Hansel in her oven. Stick to hearty meals and leave the breadcrumbs for the birds.

My Road to Hell Was Paved with Psychics

When I was at my lowest, I blew $12,000 on psychic hotlines. I'd just found out that my boyfriend was cheating on me with my neighbor, and I felt so out of control, I spiraled into a soul-sucking obsession. Not only had he cheated, but he also gave me scabies! I remember standing there with white medicated lotion slathered from head to toe feeling bewildered and absolutely devastated. With my arms up like a Ken doll, I sobbed in front of the mirror, asking my reflection, *Isn't scabies a thing only pirates get?* I had more questions, which led me down a rabbit hole of obsession. *Why did he cheat on me? Is it because the neighbor is a successful lawyer with six-pack abs? Why don't I have six-pack abs? Clearly, he left me because I'm fat. If I lose weight, will my boyfriend change his ways and beg to come back to me? Am I that unlovable? How do I make myself lovable?*

I would call a psychic, ask them my obsessive questions, and if I got an answer I didn't like, I'd hang up and call another one. I became a psychic junkie. On top of that, my eating disorder was in full swing. I'd lost thirty pounds in thirty days.

I found myself back in that cold, sterile void originally left by my father, discarded and alone. Only this time, instead of beginning my life, I was on my way to ending it. At this point, I'd developed full-on OCD (obsessive-compulsive disorder), a condition that traps you in a cycle of rumination and uncontrollable invasive thoughts and behaviors that are stuck on repeat, and you can't stop. I wasn't sleeping, wasn't eating, and I couldn't stop obsessing over being discarded and feeling inferior. I felt so worthless, I wanted to die.

Feeling like shit became my addiction. It was like emotional self-harm. My brain seemed to be hooked on the self-pity that swirled around in my head. I wallowed in my suffering, obsessing over my ex, constantly checking his social media, and feeling powerless to stop making myself miserable. There's a scientific name for emotional self-harm. In psychology, they refer to it as "cognitive distortions." According to Harvard Health, cognitive distortions are internal dialogues, negative emotional filters, or mental biases that make us feel like shit about ourselves and the world.

Rumination is a common thing the brain does when it's trying to solve a problem. We all do it to a certain extent. But rumination combined with cognitive distortions create a recipe for disaster. In my head, I have many cognitive distortion divas whispering outrageous and sometimes cruel things to me. I call them my "Trauma Divas." Most of us have that voice in our minds that tells us we aren't good enough. Sometimes it's several voices. Maybe one has the voice of a parent who always belittled you. Perhaps another was born out of a traumatic event and became hypervigilant to keep you from being harmed again. Another might be from an obsessive place that worries and frets about every little thing. If we're not careful, we could find ourselves taking these voices too seriously. We may even start to believe what they're saying. That's why I gave my critical inner voices outlandish personas, to make it easier for me to identify them and laugh at what they say.

Trauma Divas

Here they come, strutting in all their glory onto a spectacular drag show stage. Put your hands together for the Trauma Divas! Please welcome:

- Catastrophe Jane

  Catchphrase: Just waiting for the other stiletto to drop.

  - This bitch has a knack for blowing things way out of proportion and overreacting to everything. She tells me things like, "Ohmyfuckinggod! This is the worst thing that has ever happened to us! Our lives are over! Ruined! Burn it all down! Aaaaaaaaagh!"

- Black-and-White Betty

  Catchphrase: I got two switches at my disposal: breaking bottles and lighting things on fire or off-the-grid false serenity, baby.

  - She's an emo queen that sulks around and commonly uses the words *always, never, nobody,* and *everybody.* She listens to Snow Patrol and cries, "Nobody loves us. Everybody abandons us. We'll always be alone, and we'll never find anyone to love us."

- Miss Chaos Cleo

  Catchphrase: Call me now to feel even shittier about yourself.

  - This broke-down psychic's got a 99 Cent Store crystal ball and a passion for bad fortune telling. Miss Chaos Cleo predicts a grim future. She'll say things like, "Your ex is probably having the best time of his life with your neighbor. They're going to have a beach wedding and have, like, a dozen children. My senses are telling me they laugh about you when they're together."

- Pissy Peggy

  Catchphrase: Get your umbrella, bitch, 'cause Peggy's here to piss on your parade!

  - If this diva finds out anything positive you did, she'll find a way to golden shower all over it. Most of her sentences start with "Yeah, but" or "Only." For instance, if I got hired for a big modeling job, Pissy Peggy will say, "Yeah but you didn't book the Calvin Klein job." If a hot guy showed interest in me, she would prance in and say, "He only likes you because he doesn't know who you truly are yet."

- Lucy Labeler

  Catchphrase: I'm like a hard-on, honey, I give it to you straight.

  - If you like insulting yourself and spending hours being an emotional punching bag, Lucy's the diva for you. She'll label you as "fat," "ugly," or "worthless" on a loop in your head until you really fucking hate yourself. She'll also label your dates as "Out of your league," and "Way hotter and better than you."

- Sharon Shoulda

  Catchphrase: Your good ain't good enough. You shoulda done better!

  - If you're feeling particularly good about yourself or even just adequate, Sharon's ready to should (shit) all over your joy. She'll remind you of all the things you should be doing, even when you need and deserve a rest. She'll "should" the bed before you can lie down in it. She says things like, "You should work out more," or if you're having a nice date, "You should stop talking so much so he doesn't get bored of you." Sharon's a real should storm.

- It's All About Me Mabel

  Catchphrase: But enough about you . . .

  - Mabel's talent is to take something that has absolutely nothing to do with you and make it all about you. She'll take anything personally. If your date has to cancel due to an emergency, she'll whisper, "He doesn't really have an emergency; he just doesn't want to date you." If someone ghosts you, she'll write a ten-page manifesto on everything you said and did wrong to make them not want to be with you. She centers herself harder than the sun in the solar system.

Baby, Break These Chains of Thought

In all seriousness, I knew if I didn't reach out for help, my Trauma Divas were going to get the best of me. So I found a therapist who specialized in OCD and eating disorders. With determination and patience I learned the only way to break the chain of runaway OCD thoughts is to understand the first link, the thought that starts the whole process, and then break that thought chain. As soon as I notice the first thought in that chain, I break it by saying "Stop!" out loud. If I'm in public, I'll say it under my breath or in my mind. It's important for me to pay attention and stay on top of my thoughts so I can catch myself before the thought chain goes too far.

Break the Thought Chain

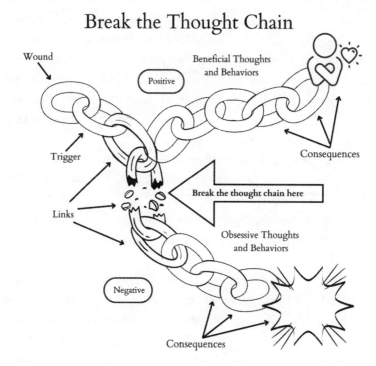

Exposure Response Prevention

For those of you who need a more clinical approach and professional intervention with obsessive thinking, there is a method called Exposure Response Prevention. ERP is a kind of behavioral therapy that safely exposes people in a gradual way to things that would activate obsession within their minds. Once that obsessive part of the brain is activated, the therapist and patient can work on reducing the distressing thoughts and situations. It helps the patient cope with triggers and practice taking charge to prevent their compulsion from overriding the system. For someone like me, that might look like my therapist asking me why I keep bringing up my ex. I would tell my therapist what obsessive thoughts were presenting themselves, and then we would work to reduce the magnitude of those thoughts. She gave me tools, such as the breaking the thought chain, to help me get in control of those obsessive thoughts.

While this kind of therapy doesn't completely eliminate the obsessive thinking, it does provide a way to manage those thoughts so they don't interfere with my life.

Obsessive thoughts lead to obsessive actions. But you don't have to stay in that loop. One trick I learned is that when you're going through a hard time, take fifteen minutes to grieve really hard. After fifteen minutes, let it go. I got this from a TV show, and it may be the best advice I've ever heard. Another way to take charge of obsessive thinking is to pay attention to your thoughts and make sure you have tools in place to help you manage them, such as the chain-breaking tool. If we're not paying attention, our brains cycle repetitive thoughts through our minds on autopilot. Even though we're not paying attention, those thoughts still have an impact on how we view ourselves and the world. For things like Exposure

Response Therapy, it's important to have a professional therapist with experience to guide you through the process. Don't try to do it alone. It's also a good idea to make sure you have the support of your friends and family. Discuss your triggers with safe people so they can help you through the obsessive thoughts whenever possible.

Instead of allowing myself to obsess over someone else, I started focusing on myself. I paid attention to the thoughts spurred by my Trauma Divas and stopped them before they roped me into the obsessive-compulsive chain. My therapy journey was a long road, which is why it will take more than one chapter to cover it. I've had to face some terrifying and difficult truths, which included examining my past fuckboy experiences, like the one with the Mama's Boy.

A Fuckboy Only a Mother Could Love

When I first started dating this mama's boy (a.k.a. Man-Child from the Wall of Shame), I was fairly new to dating men. I met him on a dating app, and he seemed like such a nice guy. He had no idea that I was newly out of the closet, and I didn't think to mention it. So when he googled me and saw my interviews relating to my advocacy work in which I mentioned having a girlfriend, he had some questions. I told him that was my past and it was nobody's business, which he seemed to accept. He did more than accept it; he was full-on love bombing me, saying things like, "Oh my gosh, I've never met a guy like you before. My mom is going to love you!"

When he wasn't love bombing me, he couldn't stop talking about his mom and his family. Honestly, I'm a mama's boy too. But there's a difference between an independent mama's boy and a codependent mama's boy. One has a healthy relationship with his mother, the other has an unhealthy dependence on his mom that dominates his life. My date was definitely the codependent mama's boy. Everything he did and every decision he made was centered on his mother. His mom approved or disapproved of his boyfriends, told him when to go to bed at night, and when to get up in the morning. It wasn't just his mother. His sister also had to approve of his dating choices. They didn't approve of his ex-boyfriend, which left a spot for me in the hot seat.

Mama's Boy insisted on picking me up from the airport on Thanksgiving weekend, which, if you know the nightmare that is the Los Angeles International Airport, is a huge deal, especially on a holiday weekend.

I remember thinking, "I can't believe he's picking me up from the airport. This must mean we're taking our relationship to the next level."

We'd never even fully hooked up yet, and he was ready to brave the traffic and stress of one of the most annoying and busiest airports in the country. After he picked me up, I took him to dinner. I had this nagging feeling that something was off, but I couldn't place it. My suspicions were confirmed the next day when he vanished. I was texting him, asking if everything was okay, and got no response. It was so bizarre, because he'd just picked me up from the airport (he'd taken the 405!). I couldn't help but wonder, did his mom tell him to dump me?

After a few weeks had passed, he found out that I was searching for a home to buy. He had the audacity to reach out to me and recommend his mother as my Realtor. "My mom is the best in the business," he said without a shred of self-awareness. Even in our breakup, his mom was right in the center.

Trot Out Your Trauma Divas

Who are your Trauma Divas?

Do they have a catchphrase? What's the thing they say in a loop in your mind?

Examples: What's the point? I'm never good enough. Nobody likes me. I don't belong, etc.

Write down each trauma diva, giving them funny names to help you dismiss the lies they are telling you. Now write a quick response to each trauma diva, such as The point is to enjoy life. I like who I am. My home is with me.

Print your responses and put them up as affirmations around your home or at your desk so you can see them every day.

FUCKBOY LESSON *Number Four*

Sometimes our own mind lies to us just as much as (or more than) fuckboys do. It might make you believe the world is ending or that you're worthless when it's not and you're not. Ask yourself if what you're thinking is really true. Fuckboys can spot someone who lies to themselves from a mile away.

Looking back on the Mama's Boy story, I realize how much I relied on others for my happiness. When he was love bombing me, I was on top of the world. It was an exhilarating feeling and I never wanted it to end. But love bombing is not sustainable, and it did end. In a way, I was doing the same thing as the Mama's Boy. He put his destiny in the hands of his mother and sister, and I was putting my destiny in the hands of the men I dated.

In order to fill my mind with helpful, constructive thoughts, I first needed to clear out the clutter of obsessive thoughts. As a person who's struggled with OCD, this was challenging, but I can tell you that it is doable. When we let our Trauma Divas run the show, we end up with a toxic cocktail of catastrophe, negativity, self-pity, bad predictions of tragedy, chaos, shaming, and black-and-white thinking. This can lead to a whole host of self-reinforcing negative behaviors, such as stalking your ex on social media, indulging in addictions, wallowing, and isolation. It's never a good idea to put your Trauma Divas in charge.

After I quieted the noise of obsessive thinking, I was able to ask myself what I truly wanted. I wanted to be happy. But it took me a while to understand that only I can be in charge of my happiness. Before I could even begin to take charge of my happiness, I needed to identify what that means for me.

PART TWO

HEALING, PARTY OF ONE

CHAPTER FIVE

Reframing the Fuckboy

"Fuck you! How dare you not see how amazing Peter is! He's the nicest guy you'll ever meet. And you're a piece of shit."

There I was, at a gay bar, staring at this woman I'd never seen before, and she was screaming at me about a guy I'd recently ended things with. "Uh, who are you?" I asked.

"I'm his wife!" She screeched. I looked over and saw Peter in the corner, bawling his eyes out. His wife ran back to him, cradled his head in her lap, and glared at me from across the room.

Fucking West Hollywood, I thought. At this point, I was in my thirties and did not have the patience for this level of drama. The irony is, I had tried to make it work because he was such a nice guy. I hadn't ghosted him; I just realized life is too short to pretend you're into someone when you're not. I respectfully told him I wasn't feeling it and that I was sorry. It was wonderfully uncomplicated. Little did

I know, he was also married to a woman the whole time. So, a little more complicated than I thought.

Maybe They're Coffee and You're Tea

One dreary autumn day, I remember sitting in my therapist's office obsessing about a guy who had ghosted me, ruminating about everything we did, wondering where it all went wrong.

Suddenly, my therapist interrupted me. "Ryan, maybe they prefer coffee and you're tea." This simple thought had never occurred to me and was a complete game changer.

In the past when a guy ghosted me, I would take it so personally. I'd obsess over why he didn't want to talk to me or be with me. *Maybe it's because of my body size. Did I say something wrong? Maybe he likes someone more attractive.* This would go on and on in my head, and it was exhausting. The truth is it was none of my business why they weren't into me. It was clear that the real issue had nothing to do with the fuckboys who were ghosting me and everything to do with my OCD.

Without getting too clinical, here's a quick rundown on obsessive-compulsive disorder. OCD is an anxiety disorder that causes intrusive thoughts and obsessions and repetitive, sometimes ritualistic behaviors. When it comes to love and relationships, there are a few obsessions that may occur:

- Limerence: involuntarily hyperinfatuation with someone or, as Psych Central puts it, "acute longing for emotional reciprocation, obsessive-compulsive thoughts, feelings and behaviors, and emotional dependence on another person."

- Erotomania: when someone suffers from the delusion that a person of a higher status, such as a celebrity, is in love with them.

- Obsessive love disorder: an extreme obsession with someone, causing excessive controlling or protective behavior.

- Love addiction: excessive attraction and infatuation with one or more love interests that causes a lack of control, disconnection from friends, family, and interests, and unhealthy attachments in romantic relationships.

My particular brand of obsession was a torturous cocktail of limerence and love addiction with a healthy splash of rumination and garnished with a giant wedge of self-hatred. It tasted like tears, regret, and shame. Until I became conscious of these obsessions, I was doomed to repeat the cycle.

It would go something like this: I'd meet a guy and immediately start fantasizing about our lives together (limerence). We'd go out and I would find myself in weird situations in which I would completely abandon or betray myself by doing things that made me feel uncomfortable, not enforcing my boundaries, not even having boundaries, staying when I wanted to leave, and so on (love addiction). Then, regardless of whether I was into the guy, if he ghosted me, I'd tell myself terrible stories about why he'd disappeared (rumination). All the focus was on me and my flaws. It was never about the other person.

On top of that, I always felt like I had to get the last word in during conversations, especially via text. Even if no response was necessary, I was compelled to write or say something, anything to get the last word. One day, my therapist asked me, "Why do you feel like you have to get the last word?"

I had to stop and think. *Why do I feel that way?* Then it hit me. "Because he's not going to remember me." There it was. All my fear stemming all the way back to my childhood. I'm afraid I'll be forgotten because my father's absence made me believe I'm unremarkable and unlovable. I desperately wanted to leave a lasting impression. My OCD was rooted in my fear of abandonment. When I was ghosted, it triggered that fear of abandonment, leaving me drowning in a puddle of my own insecure thoughts.

"Maybe you could let the last word go," my therapist suggested. So, what then? Just don't respond? It took me a while to fully grasp what my therapist was trying to say. Then I overcorrected, swinging the opposite direction, and becoming way too unresponsive, which led to more ghosting. The guys I dated thought I just didn't give a fuck. This landed me back in my therapist's office, shaking my head.

The Hot Mess Express—All Aboard!

"Why haven't I heard from him in two days—"

"Stop right there," my therapist would say. "Stop the thought train. Break the chain before it leads to a runaway train of obsessive thoughts." This image was just what I needed to get out of my obsession. The trick for me was to figure out the thought that jump-started my obsessive thought train and stop if before it starts. This sounds simple, but it's also difficult. I had to find specific thoughts to counter the initial thought in the runaway train that was my Hot Mess Express (see "Breaking the Thought Chain" in chapter four). For instance:

> *It's fine if they don't like me. I'll be okay.*
> *Not everyone has to like me.*

I don't like everyone. Why would I expect everyone to like me?
Did I even really like this person?
Eh, maybe he's coffee and I'm tea.
It's fine if he's not calling. Take it for what it is. Maybe he's
    not into me. No big deal.
And eventually, *Oh, fuck it. Next!* (This was during my
    fuckboy era).

For some who have OCD, nothing is more titillating than obsession. This obsession tied me to the train tracks on the route to Chaos
Town. Simultaneously, I was the damsel in distress, the villain who
tied me to the tracks, and the conductor about to run my ass over.
All aboard! If I wasn't directly in a chaotic situation in any given
moment, my brain would create inner chaos because that's what felt
familiar. My tendency toward emotional self-harm made it almost a
habit, obsessing about my body, emotionally abusing myself, tying
myself to the railroad tracks and running myself over with my obsessive thought trains. If I was really going to stop the thought trains, I
needed to confront my desire to cause myself harm.

Best Friend Versus Worst Enemy

Imagine going through a breakup and sitting with your best friend,
looking for a bit of love and sympathy. What if, instead of being
supportive and compassionate, your best friend says, "Well, he probably dumped you because of your body." As you look at her in disbe-
lief, she hits you again with, "You're super unremarkable. I bet
they've already forgotten about you." As if that's not bad enough, she
deals a final blow, "I wonder if anyone will ever love you."

Chances are, you'd find a new best friend. Yet I would think these
things about myself every time a relationship or situation-ship didn't

work out. I was sleeping with the enemy . . . in my mind, and that bitch never took the night off.

My mental self-torture came from a protective place within me, one that didn't want me to need the love or affection of anyone. The cocktail of drama chemicals swirled in my brain, lighting up familiar neurological patterns and intoxicating me in the worst way. I berated myself and wallowed in the alluring embrace of self-loathing until, eventually, my need for a new supply of outside validation forced me to find someone else to treat me on the outside the way I felt I deserved on the inside. It was a twisted and vicious cycle.

There came a point when I knew I had to put down the thousand-pound weight of shame and self-hatred that I'd been carrying for decades. Hating myself was exhausting, and it wasn't doing me any good. It certainly didn't make the drama go away. I realized that if I wanted my outside dating circumstances to change, I needed to change how I felt on the inside. But it didn't happen overnight.

My road to self-love didn't start with becoming my own best friend. The shift was more subtle at first. Instead of self-love, I switched to apathy. I just stopped giving a fuck. You want to ghost me? Who cares! Next! You want to take it a little further and start a relationship? Eh, not that into it. Next! You want to be a fucking weirdo? Byeeeeee. Next! Apathy gave me so much freedom. When I was finally able to put down that thousand-pound weight, I became the fuckboy, and that felt fucking amazing . . . for a while. I suddenly had the power because I didn't fucking care anymore. And during my fuckboy era, I realized it was never about me when someone ghosted me. In fact, it was none of my fucking business what they thought of me or why they weren't into me. In my fuckboy era, I wasn't breaking things off because of the person I was dating. I was leaving because I wasn't in a place to have a relationship. I ended things with dates because they just weren't my cup of tea. I wanted to have fun without all the stress, self-pity, and inner turmoil. That was the beginning of a new chapter for me.

Hard Pass

An interesting thing happened when I stopped obsessing over guys. I discovered there were things I was no longer willing to tolerate. The first time I realized I even had a deal-breaker was when I was at a club with my friend. She had introduced me to an acquaintance while we were on the dance floor. The music was loud, so he didn't think I could hear him when he leaned over and shouted into my friend's ear, "He's too fat for me. I don't date fat guys." Right then, I decided I would never date someone who body-shamed me or judged me because of my body size. As my self-worth grew, I developed a full list of deal-breakers:

Deal-Breakers

Body-shamers

My ex-girlfriend body-shamed me all the time. She would actually say out loud that her ex had a better body than me. The guy at the club was a trigger for a deep and familiar wound, and I was finally able to say, "No more."

In the closet

I learned about this one when a guy I was dating, who was in the closet, cheated on me. And the person he cheated with was the guy who helped him decide to come out of the closet. It felt like shit to know I wasn't good enough for him to declare his sexuality but that this new guy was so amazing, my ex burst through the closet doors. This is a common issue in the gay community, when someone's ex comes out of the closet and they wonder, "Was I not good enough?"

Already taken

Someone who is already in a relationship but also wants to date me. I used to justify it and believe them when they said they were "kind of ending things." Never again!

Liars

Need I say more about this?

Belittlers

When people talk down to me, that's a hard pass. The Canadian fuckboy used to say, "No one thinks you're funny," and other belittling phrases. Anyone who makes me feel like shit about myself can see themselves all the way out of my life.

Gaslighters

Gaslighting makes me question everything that happens to me, which is terrible for my OCD tendencies. My ex-girlfriend used to gaslight me all the time, and it made me insane.

Drug users

I am *not* into guys who do hard drugs. I don't want a partner who's going to drop dead from a fentanyl overdose.

Deal-Breakers Versus Growing Pains

How do we define a deal-breaker? And how do we separate deal-breakers from growing pains?

Sometimes a fear of intimacy may manifest as a long list of deal-breakers and a set of standards that are impossible for any human to meet. Unrealistic deal-breakers often serve as protection for someone who struggles to be vulnerable with a romantic prospect, and so, it's important to distinguish deal-breakers from normal relationship growing pains.

What is a deal-breaker?

I define it as a nonnegotiable. It's something you recognize right away as harmful to you and makes you want to get the fuck out of there immediately.

What is a normal relationship growing pain?

I see a growing pain as something that might make you uncomfortable but that could be worked out with honest, vulnerable communication or adjusting your expectations. For instance, if your partner is kind and loving but too passive and never takes the initiative, an open conversation may help you find a solution that benefits you both.

Is it really a deal-breaker?

Let's say, for example, someone has bad teeth. Is that *really* a deal-breaker? Or is that something you could get past if they are a good person who meets your romantic needs? Maybe you'll get used to it (or maybe they'll find an amazing dentist). When making your list of deal-breakers, be sure not to be too picky. Allow room for minor flaws and shortcomings.

THE ONLY REASON I know what my deal-breakers are is because I experienced the fallout from these things directly and decided I'd had enough. It's important for us to learn our own lessons and set our own limits at our own pace. Sometimes a person needs to experience consequences more than once to finally get it. For instance, I knew the minute I met my good friend's date that he was a fuckboy and tried to warn her. After they hooked up, she didn't hear from him for a few days.

"When should I text him?"

"Never." I said. "Pump the brakes, sister. This guy was claiming to be so into you, and he hasn't talked to you in days. Why would you want a relationship with him?" Sure enough, after about a week, he texted her asking her to Venmo him money for a poker game. Now, that's *her* deal-breaker. A guy who asks you for money after neglecting you . . . that is never going to end well.

I've asked my friends about their deal-breakers, and many of them, as they started listing them off, realized the person they were dating had at least one of their deal-breakers in play. We've all been programmed in one way or another to accept things without thinking too much about them. It's not until we bring conscious awareness to these things that we can leave and stay gone when deal-breakers are present. For those with repeat offenders in their lives, ask yourself, *Why do I keep going back when I see the red flags and I should be running as far away as possible?* A therapist may be able to help you become aware of your deal-breakers and figure out why you ignore or overlook red flags. A sign of a healthy person is to leave when red flags or deal-breakers are present and never look back.

Intimate Partner Deal-Breakers

Sometimes, deal-breakers don't show up until you've been in a relationship with someone for a while. That's another good reason to occasionally check in with and reevaluate your deal-breaker list. Your list for when you first meet someone may be different than it is for an intimate partner.

Intimate partner deal-breaker traits may include:

- Emotionally abusive
- Physically abusive
- Cheating (sometimes that's not a deal-breaker, and that's okay, no judgment)
- Doesn't contribute to shared responsibilities (financial, social, chores, emotional)
- Gaslighting
- Manipulative (liar)
- Controlling

We must be clear on what we will and will not tolerate in all relationships. If you have your list memorized, it will be easy to spot red flags so you can avoid problematic relationships before they even start (hopefully). Guard these deal-breakers. Many people hide their true colors at the beginning of relationships. I say you don't really know who you're dating until about the three-to-six-month mark. If you're dating a psycho who knows your deal-breakers, they may temporarily refrain from doing those things while love bombing you to get you hooked on those feel-good love chemicals before they reveal themselves.

It should also be noted that deal-breakers are different from boundaries. Boundaries can be helpful in relationships. They can actually bring couples closer together because there is an understanding of expectations and a mutual respect. Deal-breakers are like the emergency ripcord. You pull it when you want to eject yourself from the situation immediately. That may be more difficult if the relationship has lasted longer, so do what's best for you and exit at your own pace. But I recommend keeping your list of deal-breakers with you, if you have to, so you can remind yourself of the shit you won't tolerate and date accordingly.

While I had a solid list of my deal-breakers, and I was learning to stop obsessing over guys who ghosted me, my dating life still had a few bumps in the road. One bump in particular, showed me the importance of respectfully ending things instead of ghosting. For that lesson, I have the Thirty-Year-Old Virgin to thank.

The Thirty-Year-Old Virgin

When we went out for drinks, he told me right away that he was a virgin. To be honest, I thought it was admirable. Maybe this was just the guy I needed. We talked every day and had some amazing make-out sessions. Not only was he super cute, but we were definitely vibing, and I'm pretty sure he felt the same way. It was going great, until our third date.

We got takeout and watched a movie. One thing led to another, and we found ourselves making out in my bedroom. I knew to take things slow, since he was a virgin. But the intensity of this make-out session was insane. The intimacy was building, and I could feel a powerful connection. I know he felt it too, perhaps a little too much, because he suddenly pulled away.

"I have to go home," he said.

This surprised me because we'd planned for him to spend the night at my place.

"Oh, okay, sure." I walked him out and didn't hear from him for the rest of the night. I told my friend what happened. "I'm for sure never hearing from this guy again," I told my friend. "It's done, it's over." But I was wrong.

The next day, to my surprise, he texted me a sweet and sincere message, telling me how much he enjoyed hanging out with me. "I'm just in a place where I can't date right now." He had just been in a serious relationship and was still recovering.

First of all, this was completely new territory for me. He didn't ghost me? I didn't have to spend days and weeks wondering what happened, obsessing over what I did wrong, and creeping on his social media for clues? What? While it wasn't the answer I'd hoped for, at least I had my answer. Sure, I was disappointed that we couldn't take the relationship further. But he gave me closure. "I totally understand, and I really appreciate your message. Maybe our paths will cross in the future," I texted back.

This ending helped me to see that it's not personal. Not only that, but it's none of my business why it's not working for someone in the early stages of a relationship. It doesn't have to be that deep. It could just be that he's a coffee guy, and I'm not his cup of tea. This perspective changed the way I interacted in all of my future dating relationships. When I got ghosted, I stopped taking it personally. When I wasn't feeling a relationship, I did the right thing and broke it off respectfully instead of ghosting.

Determine Your Deal-Breakers

- Have you ever been heartbroken?

- If yes, what happened? Fill in the blank, such as:

- They cheated

- Body-shamer

- Belittler

- They were in the closet

- Others (list below)

_____

_____

_____

_____

_____

It's important to note that there are pre-relationship deal-breakers and then there are those you discover during relationships. Constantly reevaluate your deal-breakers. Your list will continue to grow as you date more people or go deeper in your relationships.

FUCKBOY LESSON *Number Five*

> *Your mind can be your best friend or your worst enemy. You get to decide.*

With the peace I felt after healing my tendency toward rumination, I was able to examine what exactly I was looking for in a relationship. Instead of obsessing over ghosts, I looked to the horizon. I got clear about what I wanted out of future relationships. Sure, I had a list of deal-breakers, but what about a list of the things I want, as well as what I don't want? I decided to create a dating scale to measure my dates based on my values and not just if they had six-pack abs and a nice smile.

CHAPTER SIX

What Does Happy Feel Like?

There was this guy who was on the cover of magazines. He'd been on television and big city billboards. He was flirty, had nice friends, and was always up for a dating adventure. He had grown weary of being ghosted all the time, and so he decided to flip the script and be the one to do the ghosting. He became a fuckboy. Hi. I'm the fuckboy. It's me.

Six years ago, I was getting to know a guy who lived across the country but was planning on moving to Los Angeles within weeks. Our FaceTime calls were phenomenal. We talked every day, and he was so excited to connect when he got to LA. But when he did, I ignored his texts, calls, and emails. I unequivocally ghosted him. We'd invested so much time and emotion talking via FaceTime, but when the moment came for us to meet in the flesh, I said, "Fuck it," and disappeared from his life forever. It had nothing to do with him.

I was afraid that when he saw me in person, he wouldn't find me attractive.

Fast-forward to 2023, I was at a bar in West Hollywood with three friends. We were seated communally, where more than one party shares a table. As we were enjoying our cocktails, the hostess brought over a party of six to join us. That's when I heard my name. "Hi, Ryan."

I looked up and there he was, the FaceTime hottie I'd ghosted. His friend asked how we knew each other, and he just came right out and said it. "Oh, Ryan ghosted me a few years ago." I was mortified, swimming in shame over being the jerk who led him on and then ghosted him. I also couldn't help but wonder what might have happened if I hadn't blocked him. It occurred to me that I had no idea how much I may have hurt the guys I'd ghosted during my fuckboy phase, or how long it would take them to forget about it. The FaceTime hottie was pleasant and even said it was great to see me when he got up to leave.

I learned from that embarrassing experience that it's always more dignified to end things respectfully than it is to ghost someone. I was swimming in so much insecurity, I couldn't see a way to get out of meeting the FaceTime hottie. As we've established, my ghosting him had nothing to do with him and everything to do with me. The model I had for relationships was skewed when my father ghosted me. I was never taught how to walk away from a person while keeping the dignity on both sides intact. This is a skill I had to learn, and it wasn't easy.

Everything in my body would be screaming, "Get out! Run!" as if the building were on fire. Ending things respectfully had to begin with regulating my emotions.

If you are thinking of ending things with someone, make sure you are calm. Do some yoga, take some breaths, and wait until your body is relaxed. To regulate your emotions, ask yourself if you're really in danger. If the answer is no, remind yourself that you are safe. If it helps, repeat to yourself, *I am safe. I am safe. I am safe.* Look around at your environment to prove to yourself that you are not in danger. Are you in your cozy home? Are you outside near nature? Look for all the ways that you are safe. Once you convince your nervous system that you are safe, look for the beauty around you. Notice colors, textures, light, sounds, anything that brings you peace.

This doesn't have to be a major meditation event. For someone who is constantly managing emotional dysregulation, I need to be able to do this anywhere. It's a quick calming technique that brings my body back to neutral so I can make good decisions from a place of calm, rather than panic. From this space, I am able to use sound judgment that honors the dignity of myself and others when I need to end a situation-ship that's run its course.

How to Get Out of a Situation-Ship—a Break-Up Guide for the Conflict Averse

If you're a human being, it's impossible to avoid conflict. Still, some of us would rather swallow bees than engage in a difficult discussion. The truth is, whether you ghost someone or end things respectfully, it's going to hurt either way. The only difference is, when you ghost, you don't see the pain you've caused. But it still exists, and it will affect you, somehow and someway. It's better to learn how to respectfully rip those situation-ship Band-Aids off. Depending on how long you've been dating, there are several ways to go about it:

ONE TO THREE Months—This early in the situation-ship, no one is owed a long explanation as to why this isn't working. The less time you've spent together, the more acceptable it is to end things via a text that says something like:

> I appreciate the time we've spent together, but this isn't working for me. I've decided to move on. I wish you the best. Please take care.

They may ask why, but at this stage, you don't owe them an explanation. If they persist, the block button is your friend.

THREE TO SIX MONTHS—A breakup text at this stage is rude and insensitive. At the three-to-six-month mark, your date deserves a phone call. It doesn't need to be a long conversation, but you will need to assert yourself. You could say something like:

> We've had some fun together, but I don't see this going anywhere for me personally. I hope we can continue to be friends, but if that's not an option for you, I respect that and wish you the best.

If they demand more of an explanation, keep it short and focused on you. You could say something like:

> I'm not interested in pursuing this any further because of my own personal reasons, and I hope you understand.

Then end the conversation. Prolonging it at this point will only exacerbate the awkwardness and pain for both of you.

SIX MONTHS AND Up—Only an epic jerk would ghost after this point. Grow a spine and break up in person.

Important distinction! Only break up in person if it is safe to do so. If the person is abusive, it's okay to break up via phone or email to protect yourself. Make sure you have support and are in a safe place where they can't harm you.

When breaking up with someone at this stage of the relationship, it might be best to pick a public place to minimize a long and drawn-out spectacle. Your conversation will be more specific to your relationship at this stage. At this point, you'll know the person pretty well and should be able to find the words to respectfully break up while minimizing the damage. But here is an example of something to get the conversation started:

> While I've enjoyed the time we've spent together, I don't want to move forward with this relationship. I think it's best if we part ways. Please know that I wish you all the best. This just isn't working for me.

It may be tempting to stay and take care of their feelings after you've said the difficult thing, but don't linger for too long. Not only will you be unable to ease their pain, but you may give them false hope that you'll want to make the relationship work. Let them go to their friends for support.

It may take some getting used to, but it's way more dignified to say, "I'm just not into this," than to ghost. Don't be that asshole. Not only will you have more respect for yourself, but you'll also avoid potential awkward encounters down the road if you run into this person again. Ghosts linger, and they always come back to haunt us.

From Fucked Boy to Fuckboy

When overwhelming heartbreak left me feeling jaded and devastated, my priority shifted to one thing: control. I needed to have control over my dating life, more than anything else, including true connection. I only dated "hot guys," judging potential dates based *only* on their physical appearance. Decency and sincerity flew out the fuckboy window, and my mission was to use men the way they'd used me. But at least I was a Well-Intended Fuckboy . . . wasn't I?

Well-intended or not, I thoroughly enjoyed my new, powerful fuckboy persona. But when my therapist asked me if I was happy, I was stumped. I literally had no idea how to answer that question. "What even *is* happy?" I responded, and I sat in stunned silence. Everyone says that they want happiness, but what does happy feel like? Can a jaded fuckboy be happy? My therapist and I dug deep and began to find an answer together: happiness, for me, feels like contentment, being at peace with my life, my job, my relationships, and my body. Based on this this metric, no, I wasn't happy yet. But I was starting to believe I could get there. Or at least I hoped I would.

What Does Happy Feel Like to You?

Write down your answer here.

Before I could even begin to address my fuckboy tendencies, I needed to go further back. I'm talking way back, to the first time I binged on food. If I'm being honest, that is where my unhealthy coping mechanisms began. When I got real with myself about my binge eating disorder, it opened a world of truth that I didn't even realize existed.

My Original Obsession

The first time I binged, I was thirteen years old. My mom and her boyfriend took us out to a restaurant, and before the food had even come out, I ate six loaves of bread. "Oh, he's just a growing boy," my mom said. The truth was, I had tragically low self-esteem and was hiding a lot of pain. Food lowered the volume on the hateful comments around me and the self-hatred within me. I'd struggled with body image since I was young. I remember wearing a T-shirt in the pool at eight years old because I was self-conscious about my body. Food became my comfort, temporarily shielding me from my insecurities and self-loathing.

Food never yelled or talked down to me. It was reliable, always there for me when I needed it. My compulsion to restrict after binging was just as powerful as my food cravings. At seventeen years old, I starved myself and lost eighty-five pounds in an extremely unhealthy amount of time. My doctor congratulated me. In college, instead of gaining the "freshman fifteen," I lost weight. I was still binging, but I was working out twice a day. I'd go to my friend's dorm for dinner, and while I was there, I'd go into the bathroom and call for a to-go order from the restaurant downstairs. Then, I'd leave early and pick up my order so I could eat in private.

As my binge eating disorder progressed into adulthood, I would sometimes binge ten thousand calories in one sitting, and my fast-food budget went up to seven hundred dollars per week. I'd go to dinner with friends, then on the way home, I'd hit up two or three more fast-food restaurants. In my car, I always had a designated grocery bag to hide all of the fast-food bags as I carried them into my apartment so nobody would see how much I was consuming. Binge eating was destroying my health, my finances, my self-worth, and my life. I was going into debt to fund my disorder, which only added to the shame.

Binge eating is not about being hungry. This is a common misconception. It's about obsession. For 85 percent of my day, I would think about food. I'd look up recipes at work and then late at night when I couldn't sleep, I'd get up and look at the food in my refrigerator. I would obsess about the food I wanted to eat before I got it. A rising anxiety would bubble up on my way home from work or a friend's house until I gave in and turned my car into the drive-through. There was a compulsive element at play as well. I would order the same items from each fast-food restaurant, eat them in the same order, and designate certain foods for certain spots. I had my car food, which was different from the food I ate when I got home, which was different from the food I ate when I went out with friends. When the binge eating began, it was as if I'd leave my body. That sweet momentary peace while I was eating, the dissociation—it was the high I chased with every bite as I tried to fill the cold, sterile void in my life that started with the OG (Original Ghoster), my father. But after I consumed all the food, a dark and suffocating feeling of shame would consume me, which made me hate myself all the more.

That self-loathing would lead me to the next binge, and so on, dragging me through a vicious cycle that I didn't know how to escape.

My weight fluctuated wildly as I tried desperately to pretend I was in control of my eating disorder. After a big binge, I would restrict my food intake for several days. It didn't help that I was dating a woman at the time who had anorexia. We would piggyback on each other's unhealthy behaviors. I even resorted to taking diet pills, which didn't work at all because my eating disorder had nothing to do with hunger. As a last-ditch effort, I took sleeping pills because if I was nearly comatose, I couldn't eat, right? My life had spun completely out of control.

Binge eating disorder is three times more common than anorexia and bulimia combined. Yet it wasn't recognized by the *DSM-5* (*Diagnostic and Statistical Manual of Mental Disorders*) until 2013, making it more difficult to treat before that time due to insurance restrictions. Even though men make up 25 percent of eating disorder diagnoses, and 15 percent of gay and bisexual men struggle with an eating disorder, it is rare for them to openly talk about it because of the stigma. Men don't want to seem weak, so they hide their struggle with food and don't seek help.

I hid mine for a long time, until I actually took my self-diagnosis to my therapist and said, "Hey, I think I have this." Therapists and doctors are rarely trained in medical school to screen for eating disorders, which is unfortunate because eating disorders kill a lot of people. In fact, they are among the deadliest of mental disorders. It was a relief for me when I was diagnosed with binge eating disorder. I knew that not only was this a real illness, which could be treated, but also that I wasn't alone. It was comforting to know that I wasn't the only man struggling with this. It occurs in boys and men as well as girls and women.

With my fresh new diagnosis, I started working as an advocate, sharing my story and normalizing the eating disorder struggle for men on my blog and on social media, which got a decent amount of attention. I wrote about my eating disorder on Huffington Post and *Psychology Today*. I was interviewed live on *The Today Show* in New York, and because of that appearance, I was offered an international modeling contract and became a spokesperson for the National Eating Disorders Association. I knew I was making a difference when they told me they got the highest number of calls from men on their hotline the day my interview aired. The irony is, I wasn't yet treating my own eating disorder at that time. I'd fallen into the trap of believing that the diagnosis was the cure.

I was traveling the country, doing appearances, and giving interviews, speaking in front of ten thousand people, preaching, "Love yourself!" Meanwhile, I hated myself more than ever and, in some ways, was the sickest I'd ever been. I was strutting around on stage saying, "Look at me, I'm cured!" And it was all performative bullshit. I was a total fraud. It was clear in that moment that I would surely die if I didn't take action to save myself.

Pathetic in Portugal

Toward the end of 2019, about a year and a half into my modeling career, I'd become quite successful. The irony of it all? Someone who hated his body as much as I did being paid to show it off. I was starting to see pictures of myself around town, on billboards and magazine covers, on the side of a building in New York City, and it was incomprehensible to me. My therapist asked if I was proud of my accomplishments. But instead of pride, all that came up was shame and embarrassment. The truth is, I didn't even recognize the guy on the billboards. In my mind and in the minds of a few others in the industry, living in a larger body meant I was somehow less than other models.

I was living the dream. I was getting recognition, making good money, and helping people with my eating disorder advocacy work. Yet I couldn't look at myself with anything but disgust, and I was binging more than ever.

Right around Christmas time, a client flew me to Portugal for a beach photoshoot with three other models who just happened to be drop-dead gorgeous. They'd been on the cover of *GQ* with their perfect abs and cheekbones that could cut glass. There I was, doing my best to pose for twelve hours in a bathing suit with my round, soft belly next to these beautiful men, and I felt like I was drowning. I went back to my hotel that night and called my mom, crying. I told her I felt like the token fat guy.

The modeling industry can be rough for anyone's self-esteem. But for me, a brawny model recovering from a binge eating disorder and childhood trauma, the pain was almost unbearable. I'd been devalued more than once on a modeling job. The clients would give the thinner guys better clothes, while I got the "ugly shirt," (they literally called it the ugly shirt). My agent once received an email from a client who was "concerned" that I'd gained weight over the holidays. I saw the email and vowed never to work for them again. Those microaggressions leave emotional scars that take a long time to heal.

I came home from Portugal in a full-blown existential crisis.

What am I doing? That question played on a loop in my head for weeks. In my eating disorder recovery, I wanted to be celebrating and appreciating my body. Instead, I spiraled into a hole of comparison and shame, where I couldn't even recognize myself. My therapist and I decided it would be wise for me to take a break from modeling to tend to my mental health. A few months later, the pandemic hit.

Pandemic Healing

For a lot of people, the pandemic either caused or exacerbated mental health struggles. The isolation, the uncertainty, the societal and political divides between families and friends . . . they all took a toll on our emotional and physical health. But something unexpected happened for me. Without the fear of being under the watchful eyes of friends, family, and clients, I could eat what I wanted, whenever the fuck I wanted. Food wasn't so secretive anymore. I wasn't modeling, so I didn't have to stress over weight gain. Ironically, that's when my relationship with food began to heal.

I got a new therapist who specialized in eating disorders. This therapist would have me stand in front of a mirror, every session, and ask me to say one thing that I liked about myself physically. For three months, I stood there, searching for something, just one thing, that I could honestly say I liked about my appearance. My eyes darted between my round face, my belly, my thighs, and I couldn't find any part of me that I liked. One day, out of sheer desperation, I said, "I like my nose." She asked why, and I stammered, "Because people tell me I have a good nose." In that moment I realized, I could see myself only in relation to others, through the lens of what others valued about me. But I, an international model who got paid to go overseas and have my picture taken, a person whose face was larger than life on billboards, couldn't find one thing I liked about my own appearance.

It took time and determination to see myself through a different lens. Eventually, when I looked in the mirror, away from all the noise of the rest of the world, I found reasons to love myself. I saw my soft brown eyes, my mischievous smile, my good hairline, my inviting posture, and I appreciated the person in the mirror. Without the expectations of the world on my shoulders, I began to stand tall. I stopped giving a fuck what other people thought of me.

I emerged from my post-COVID cocoon as a beautiful brawny butterfly, with a newfound appreciation for myself and my body. Since then, I've returned to modeling, and I can now see that my presence in this industry creates real value. I recognize myself and my accomplishments, and it's awesome to see my pictures in so many different places. Doing advocacy work around eating disorders as someone who has actually done the work of recovery gave me a deep sense of pride and purpose. I was also launched into a new era of dating, my fuckboy liberation tour.

What Is Happy?

After the pandemic, I was booked to do an underwear photo shoot with a major intimate apparel company. This was huge. It meant that my body would be on underwear packages at most of the major retail stores. At least when I was on billboards, I could separate myself from the image. It was so far away; it didn't even feel like me. But to have my body in a photo an arm's length away from everyone's faces was different. To say I was nervous would be an understatement.

My agent called and told me that this photo shoot was for plus-size underwear. I assumed that I would be modeling with a pair of boxers and a T-shirt. But when I arrived to set and they showed me my clothing rack, it was all briefs, boxers, and a couple of tank tops. I looked at that rack of skimpy clothing and then over to the twenty or thirty people on the set (I thought it was going to be more intimate) and took a deep breath.

Had I not done all of that healing around my eating disorder and body image over the pandemic, I would not have made it out of this alive. I reminded myself that all of these people were here to make me look good. I put on the undies and got to work.

There was a stylist pulling and tugging at my underwear, his face very close to my body, and I didn't even feel insecure. This was a huge moment for me. Not only can I look at these packages of underwear with my body displayed on the front with acceptance, but I also actually feel proud of my work. I *feel* happy.

Because for me, I realized that happiness is being able to set down my insecurities. It's about rising above the chaos in my mind, like a bird that rises above the clouds where it can't hear the busy city streets and isn't being threatened by the cars on the road.

It is pushing past all of the ways I make myself miserable.

I like a definition I found in *Psychology Today*. The article asserts that happiness is more than just a positive mood and outlook, it's a "state of well-being that encompasses living a good life, one with a sense of meaning and deep contentment." Much of our happiness is up to us.

So how do we find our happiness?

While it's great to indulge in those little pleasures in life, we can also find joy from trying new things, challenging ourselves, and giving back to our communities. *Psychology Today* has an extensive list that lays out all the signs of a happy person. My favorites are:

- Is open to learning new things and having new experiences
- Practices compassion (for self and others)
- Can be happy for others
- Doesn't hold grudges
- Doesn't play games (like ghosting or stringing people along)
- Doesn't fret over the small stuff
- Acts empowered rather than playing the victim
- Doesn't dwell on the past or worry too much about the future
- Practices generosity

What happiness comes down to for me is living a meaningful life, feeling confident and at ease with myself, letting go of the past and the small inconveniences, and staying connected to my friends, family, and community.

WHAT DOES HAPPY FEEL LIKE?

WHAT DOES HAPPY FEEL LIKE?   111

When I made progress in my healing and finding happiness, there was some sadness and regret that came up for me. I was starting to feel fully alive, and I looked back on my life and wished I'd done this healing sooner. I grieved for the younger part of myself that was stuck in suffering and misery. I kept thinking, *If only I could have freed myself before now.* But that line of thinking kept me stuck in the past, which pulled me away from the happiness I was just beginning to explore. So as an act of kindness to myself, I forgave myself for what I didn't know at the time and thanked myself for moving forward now that I have the tools to improve my life.

I love the idea of "practicing compassion." The word *practicing* implies that we don't have to do it perfectly, and that it takes work, or practice, every day. The more I practice compassion for myself and others, the more I liberate myself from old ways of thinking and feeling. That inner liberation can lead to outer liberation in the form of new and exciting encounters.

Raphael

Being a gay man can be hard on the self-esteem. It's common for gay men to get hung up on appearances. And as someone who has been in romantic relationships with both men and women, I believe that men are more visual, and they tend toward objectification more than women. That made it hard for me to let down my guard . . . until I met Raphael.

The sparks were instantaneous. I met him for coffee and couldn't take my fucking eyes off him. He was into me too; I could feel it. After our date, he walked me to my car, we hugged, and he left. Within minutes, he texted to say that he couldn't wait to see me again. He lived in New York, but his family was in California, so he made frequent trips to LA.

On a later date, he wanted to do hot yoga. I was embarrassed because I hate working out, but I decided to give it a try. After way too much sweating and awkward posing, I had to sneak out of the studio early. When he came out, all glistening and sweaty, I pretended I'd walked out just before he did. Maybe it was the exercise endorphins, but I couldn't wait to bring him back to my place. After we showered, that's when things got interesting.

As a gay man with body dysmorphia, I'd always had sex with the lights off. But Raphael wanted them on. Nervous that he would see my body, I started taking off my clothes. I almost fell over when he said, "Sit on my face." *Uh . . . what?* This had never happened before, our fully exposed bodies in the full incandescent glow of the lights, and he wants me to sit on his face? Like with my ass on his face?

I could have said no, flicked off the lights and had mediocre sex, regretting the decision forever. But instead, I said to myself, *You know what, Ryan? Enjoy yourself. You've worked hard on self-acceptance and this guy is not only hot, but clearly attracted to you. Do it!*

Gorgeous reader, let me tell you, it turned out to be one of the best sexual experiences of my life! It was the beginning of my sexual liberation. He became my sweet hook-up boy and the gateway into my own liberated fuckboy era.

Happiness List

Write a list, like the one in this chapter, but make it signs of your happiness, specifically.

- Next to each item on the list, write the ways you can bring that thing closer to you. For instance, if an item on your list is "Let go of the small things," you could write something like taking a deep breath when someone cuts me off in traffic instead of cussing them out, or saying something nice, like "Bless you!"

- Give yourself a little sticker on your list for every time you chose happiness.

- Add to your list as often as you like. You may find new ways to practice happiness as you go. Let the list change and grow, just as you are changing and growing.

— **FUCKBOY LESSON** *Number Six* —

Fucking is good, but loving yourself is better.

Sexual liberation was just one part of the equation. I was finding myself, multiple times. It took me years to realize that finding myself didn't have to be performative. True inner connection was about accepting myself, exactly as I am, no caveats, no *I'll be better or more lovable when . . .*, no false positivity. As I peeled back those performative layers, I stopped caring what other people thought. I just cared if I was happy. I realized I didn't have to prove myself to anyone. It didn't matter how many friends I had or if I was going on a date every night. The true gift of finding myself is that it allowed me to write this book, to be comfortable with going out in the world and sharing my story from a vulnerable, honest place. Finding yourself can be challenging and pretty fucking lonely and painful at times. I had to wade through my self-doubt and deep dive into difficult territories that needed healing. But the outcome is a better understanding and deeper connection with myself.

The path to finding this connection included many futile attempts to run from myself and my negative self-worth. I escaped on the binge-eating highway, then took the fuckboy express, which led me to OCD parkway, until I found myself on a small, isolated winding road that led me to loving my true self.

As with anything worthwhile, happiness is a practice. That means it requires daily effort to strengthen those happiness muscles. For some of us, the act of letting go of the small things that irritate us, like traffic or social media trolls, can be a daily practice that leads us to happier lives. For others, like me, flexing that muscle means dismantling years of pain in therapy and learning how to have compassion for myself. While there is a great deal of discomfort in this type of work, it has led me to an unexpected joy. This feeling of peace isn't easily rattled, and at its core is a love and acceptance for myself that I will never surrender again. It's too precious.

The thing is, once I found compassion and forgiveness for myself, it was also much easier to forgive all the fuckboys in my past.

CHAPTER SEVEN

It's Time for a New Scale

"So, I may be going to jail because I almost killed somebody."
That's not what you expect to hear on a third date. I suspected
nothing on our first date, when he told me he didn't drink. "I just
don't like the way it makes me feel," he lied. Honestly, who can
blame the guy? Drunken transgressions aren't usually brought up on
the first date, or even the second.

"That's perfectly fine!" I said. "I've been thinking of giving up
alcohol at this point anyway."

In the back of my mind, I wondered if he was hiding an addiction.
But who cares, as long as he's sober and in recovery now. We continued enjoying each other's company on our alcohol-free night. It
wasn't until our third date that I learned the real reason for his
sobriety.

"Listen, I've got to be honest with you," he said. "I just got out of
rehab."

No biggie, I thought.

"There's more," he said reluctantly. "On Mother's Day, I was driving down PCH [the Pacific Coast Highway]. I was drunk and I hit a parked car on the side of the road. Somebody was in that car. The impact launched them through the windshield and onto the rocks near the beach. They were hospitalized for months. I might be going to jail for a long time. I'll know more after my court date."

I didn't condone drinking and driving, even before I'd heard this story. Sure, we've all got things we regret from our past, but this had just happened, and he was still dealing with the consequences. He went to rehab because of this incident and had only been out for a month. While he was there, he had a rehab romance, so he was on the heels of a breakup and on the edge of jail. To make matters worse, he ghosted me after that date. The guy who almost killed somebody ghosted me.

Fuck this, I thought. *I need a new scale for dating.*

An Addict Is as an Addict Does

When I finally got honest with myself, I realized I was an addict too. My drug of choice? Chaos. I loved the thrill of a new toxic dating situation. What kind of crazy predicament would I fall into next? Would I make it out unscathed? (The answer was usually no . . . not without an injury, a stolen bottle of liquor, an STD, an embarrassing story that made my friends laugh, and so on and so on). Would he call or ghost me? Oh, the thrill of it all when he ghosted me for a while and *then* called me! My brain chemicals would light up as I ran through Fuckboy Forest with my hair on fire, being chased by my bad decisions. It was exhilarating . . . and so fucking toxic.

When we fall in love, our brains are flooded with a cocktail of chemicals. According to neuroscientist Stephanie Cacioppo, chemicals like dopamine (a.k.a., the "feel-good" hormone), oxy-tocin (a.k.a. the "cuddle hormone"), and adrenaline (a.k.a. the "holy shit this is awesome!" hormone), saturate and light up the pleasure centers of the brain. On top of that, our serotonin levels, which are responsible for regulating our appetite and anxiety, drop. The higher our anxiety levels, the more likely we are to become obsessed with small details, like the way our love interest words a text message.

It was clear that I was addicted to these love chemicals. But now what? How is it possible to abstain from the chemicals that flow naturally in the brain? I knew I needed a sort of love rehab but had no idea how to go about it. So I sat down with my therapist, and we mapped out a recovery plan. The first part of this plan was so simple, yet so difficult for me to figure out.

The Scale

"What are you looking for in a partner?" My therapist shifted toward me, her pen and notepad at the ready. "What do you want?" I sat, stunned, mouth agape. It was as if she'd asked me to list all the wild-life in the sea. Alphabetically.

"I don't know," I stammered. *How could I not know what I'm look-ing for in a partner?* I thought. I've been dating for six years!

This question required serious thought. Was it physical attraction I was looking for? The way I hopped from hot guy to hotter guy, one would think that looks were my top priority. But when I dug deeper, I realized my needs went way beyond the surface of a six-pack. And so my therapist and I composed a list of twenty criteria. This would become my compatibility scale.

Now, I realize some of these are absurd, but it's through the absurd that I was able to whittle it down to a solid list of five criteria that aligned with my values. I just had to wade through my own superficiality and delusions to get to the core.

My original list of twenty criteria

1. Family values
2. Solid career
3. Sense of humor
4. Honesty
5. Someone who had an amazing relationship with their father
6. How they make me feel
7. Nice eyes
8. Nice smile
9. Has money
10. Sophisticated
11. Cultured
12. Loves aviation
13. Has an above average career (lawyer, surgeon)
14. Jewish
15. No roommates
16. Nice teeth
17. Compassion
18. Empathy
19. Kindness
20. *Hot*

Obviously, this list needed some work. I had to ask myself some tough questions. For instance, how does loving aviation have anything to do with finding a compatible partner? And if a guy is everything I've been looking for but has crooked teeth, does that mean he's not the one for me? Also, if my date fits all my other criteria, but he's a nurse instead of a surgeon, am I really going to say, "Sorry, wrong scrubs for me . . ." Really? I knew I needed to radically prune this list.

I challenged myself to distill my dating criteria scale to five non-negotiable things a potential partner must have (that would actually serve my happiness and well-being) for me to even consider going on a second date.

My Five Nonnegotiables

1. Family values

2. Solid career

3. Sense of humor

4. Honesty

5. How they make me feel

Allow me to elaborate on these.

Family values

A potential partner must be someone who values family/wants to build a family. When I say "family," I believe chosen family counts just as much as blood family. This nonnegotiable is important to me because I've always dreamed of having a present, loving family. If I'm going to date someone, they must be close to their family. If they don't have any blood family or had to leave a toxic family, then they must at least have a strong relationship with friends, a.k.a., chosen family.

Solid career

I honestly don't care what they do, as long as they're passionate about it and can earn a living doing it. It doesn't have to be a great living, but at least something that can pay the bills. I want to connect with someone who understands professional ups and downs, someone I can have conversations with about work at the end of the day. It's fine if they don't understand the ins and outs of my job, but we can commiserate on work life, and I can rest at ease knowing we are both working to support ourselves.

Sense of humor

Someone who makes me laugh is crucial. Times are not always easy, but someone who can lighten the mood makes the tough times more tolerable. I'm not into people who take themselves too seriously. Life is too short for that!

Honesty

Honesty is paramount for me. I've been with too many liars, and I've come to believe once a liar always a liar. I live by Maya Angelou's words: "When someone shows you who they are, believe them the first time."

How they make me feel

This one's not necessarily about how they make me feel, but how I feel about myself when I'm around them. I don't need someone to constantly talk me up, but I do need someone who won't talk down to me. I've dated so many people who just made me feel like shit about myself, either by body-shaming me or telling me I wasn't smart/funny. But when I was around people who made me feel good about myself, I felt worthy. Of course, it took time to unlearn all the bad things I thought about myself, but once I did, I began to attract capable people who reflected back the best parts of me.

ARMED WITH MY five-item nonnegotiables list and my deal-breaker list (from the previous chapter), I was ready to test my findings in the field. So I hit the dating apps. On each date, I rated them on a scale of 1 to 7 for each category. One was the absolute worst and 7 was perfection. To be honest, hardly anybody ever got a 1 or a 7. Those numbers served as boundaries on the scale. After I rated them on each of my nonnegotiables, I would average out the score. For me to go on another date with them, they needed to score a 4 or higher. The guys who scored a 3 were at the bottom of the mediocrity barrel for me. Anyone who scored below that never worked out. I deserved someone between 4 and a 7.

Here's what each number on the scale means to me.

My Compatibility Scale

1. Train wreck
2. Red flag city
3. Meh/blah
4. I can get with this
5. Oh, damn
6. Come here, lover
7. Sliving (slaying/living your best life)

Since physical attraction wasn't on my list, I expanded my dating pool to include guys who maybe didn't have six-pack abs or a billion-dollar dynasty (more on that fuckboy later). I still dated hot guys, but an interesting thing happened when I dated according to my new scale.

Every single hot guy I dated and rated according to my scale got below a 4. When I told a friend about my scale and this grand dating experiment, she laughed and said, "You'll either come out of this with a book deal or a boyfriend, or both!" She was right.

I came out with both (more on the boyfriend later). After this extensive research in the field, I discovered a few important points.

How to Rate Your Date

Your five nonnegotiables should be unique to you. It's important to continue rating them on the scale as your relationship progresses. Keep checking in with your nonnegotiables and your deal-breakers. If one of your criteria is "good career" and you met someone who had a good job, but two months in they become unemployed and uninterested in looking for work while hinting that you should move in together, *run*. That puts them at the bottom of the scale for your "good career" criteria. It's also worth noting that the scale should evolve as you evolve. What's important to you now may not be as crucial in a year or two. As life progresses, our needs change. I find myself redefining and updating my scale on a regular basis, according to my current lifestyle and needs.

It is crucial to be honest with yourself when you're rating your dates, even if you get those passion butterflies in the beginning. If they're superhot but mean to the bartender, and one of your nonnegotiables is kindness, rate them on your scale without mercy. You're doing both of you a favor by not wasting your time. It may take a bit of practice to hone your rating skills, but once you do, you'll start seeing potential partners where you never thought to look before. The scale may seem like a limitation on your dating life, but in reality, it can open you up to a world of possibilities.

It's a Fuckboy Jungle Out There—Be Prepared!

The scale doesn't work if you don't know what you want. I've interviewed my friends, asking them the same question that stumped me in my therapist's office: "What are you looking for in a partner?" Here are some of their answers:

- Nice hands
- Great body
- Funny
- Nice eyes
- Laid back

A funny thing happened when I asked them to elaborate on their scale or asked them questions that challenged their answers. "Really?" I said to my friend who was a single mom, "Not one of the items on your list is about how your partner would treat your child, but you have 'nice hands' as a priority? So a guy with nice hands who's shitty to your kid is okay with you?" My friend hadn't even realized that she'd left off something so important.

Another friend had a pretty reasonable list. They mentioned kindness, honesty, a good job. But when I asked them to describe the last few guys they'd dated, none of them had these qualities. "Why do you think you're choosing people who don't align with your values?" I asked.

They were just as stumped as I'd been about my own dating choices.

Stepping into today's dating world requires deliberate and conscious effort. If you're not aware of what you want, how could you possibly know if the person in front of you is capable of giving it to you? If all you're looking for is "nice hands," how could you possibly expect to find someone who shares your values and treats you with respect?

Listen, it's okay if you've been unconsciously dating. Everyone's done it. When we see a pair of nice eyes and a gorgeous smile, our brains are flooded with all the feel-good chemicals, making it nearly impossible to lead with reason. But this is exactly why we must never venture into the dating wild unprepared. We must have our map (our scale) to keep us on track so we don't get lost in the fuckboy jungle with nothing but a stranger's dick in our hand.

When the Party's Over

For a long time, I struggled to create my list of nonnegotiables. But then one question brought it all into perspective for me. My mother and I are incredibly close. She's the person I trust more than anyone in the world. I know she's there when I need her. The question I asked myself is, if my mom dies, who do I want to be there for me? Who is worthy enough to become my confidant, my support, my strength, to be someone who knows me better than anyone? Is the guy I'm dating right now going to be the one I want by my side? What about everyone I'd dated in the past that I was still hung up on? That question was like a telephoto lens, magnifying and bringing everything into focus. My mom was my first experience of unconditional love, and while nobody could or should assume her role in my life, she set a standard for how I deserve to be loved. She instilled so many values in me, and along the way, I developed some of my own. Because of that bond, I know how nontransactional, pure, respectful, and sincere love feels. Her love was the foundation upon which I built my expectations. And that foundation is unbreakable.

For those of you who maybe don't have a strong bond with your parental figures, don't worry. If anyone in your life has ever demonstrated pure, unconditional love to you, you have a foundation from which to build. Even if you've never experienced it, it's perfectly okay to imagine that unconditional love and build your own foundation. Maybe for you, it's an ancestor, a movie or book character, a historical figure, or an image you've created on your own. What's important is to find the thing that brings real love into focus for you. When the party's over and the soft light of imperfect, everyday life lights up the horizon, who do you want by your side? When grief knocks you down and you can't see the good in the world, who do you want sitting next to you, holding your hand? Find the question that brings all your needs into focus. Make your scale according to that clear and vibrant picture.

All That Sparkles Isn't Love

As the elevator doors opened on the rooftop bar, our eyes locked. It was like magic. He was one of the most handsome men I'd ever seen. He was tall, polite, and incredibly smart. He spoke, like, seven different languages and went to school in China. Apparently, his family owned a multinational company, and he was worth billions. To top it all off, he agreed to meet me all the way in Santa Monica, even though he was living in West Hollywood (we've established the gesture that is dealing with the 405 freeway). I thought that was sweet at the time, until I found out the reason he didn't mind traveling. More on that later.

Our date was electric. We were connected by a gravitational pull at the center of the whole universe. The waitress even approached me while he was in the bathroom to say, "Wow, it looks like you two are having a great time and he's so good-looking! Good for you!" It felt like the whole world was rooting for us. We sat at the table, tipsy, flirting, and playing tic-tac-toe on a bar napkin until the restaurant closed.

When we walked out of the restaurant and into the sweet, salty breeze on the Santa Monica streets, he pushed me up against a wall and gave me the most passionate kiss. Sparks. Fireworks. Cheers from the whole world.

"I want to see you again." he said casually.

"How's Sunday?" I said, breathless and ecstatic that he wanted to see me again.

"Yes. Sunday." We were still floating from that hot kiss.

I never heard from him again.

Fast-forward to a year after this handsome devil ghosted me. I was at the gym, talking with my friend who worked at the front desk. She perked up, "Ryan, you won't believe who came in today . . . the billionaire!" Apparently, we go to the same gym, and he asked if she knew me. Weird. She told him we're good friends. He lied that he'd dated me. Not true. We went on *a* date . . . just one, before he ghosted me. He raved to her about what a nice guy I was, that I was attractive, and listed all the things he liked about me. I stood there, dumbfounded, waiting for her to get to the bad part. Like, what's the catch? What didn't he like about me? Did my breath stink? Was I too fat? Too desperate? What?! But that part never came. He told her that he felt bad for ghosting me, but he did it because I reminded him of his ex-boyfriend.

"Hold up," my friend interrupted him. "Let me get this straight. You ghosted Ryan because he reminded you of your ex-boyfriend, *because* he was a great guy."

"Yeah," the billionaire fuckboy said, all cute and contrite. "Do you think I should reach out to him?"

"*Nope!*" She didn't even hesitate.

"What? Why would you say that to him?" I said, resisting the urge to leap over the counter. In retrospect, she was 1,000 percent right.

Later, in a cruel act of fate, we matched on the dating app again. But by this time, I'd found out from that same friend at the gym that he was already in a relationship with someone else when we went out on that first date. That's why he wanted to meet me in Santa Monica, less likelihood that we'd run into his boyfriend.

I never spoke to him again.

Create Your Own Compatibility Scale

Write a list of twenty compatibility traits you want in a partner.

Once you have your twenty traits, narrow those down to the five most important.

This is your compatibility scale.

Now, rate your date on a scale from 1 to 7. You can use mine or create your own. Here is mine for a refresher:

1. Train wreck
2. Red flag city
3. Meh/blah
4. I can get with this
5. Oh, damn
6. Come here, lover
7. Sliving (slaying/living your best life)

Determine the lowest number your date can score in order for you to pursue the connection and act accordingly.

Feel free to update and edit your scale as you enter different eras of your life. What you find essential in your early twenties will likely change in your late twenties or early thirties. Keep checking in with yourself so you are in tune with what's important to you.

FUCKBOY LESSON *Number Seven*

"Money can't buy you class."—Countess Luanne

FINAL THOUGHTS ON THE SCALE

My obsession with the billionaire fuckboy landed me right back in my therapist's office, where we continued to refine my scale. Before that moment, I thought I was looking for a hot billionaire. But a sparkling facade couldn't hide the trash underneath. When I really examined what I actually wanted compared to the results I was getting, I realized that every hot and rich guy I dated never worked out. While they were downright intoxicating and addictive, they always led to the same place . . . with me alone, obsessing over why I'd been ghosted, stalking their social media, and sending desperate messages to "get the last word in so they don't forget about me."

This was a crucial moment. I got serious and wrote down everything that was important to me so I could figure out what I truly wanted in a partner. All my deal-breakers and all my criteria produced a clear picture of my requirements for a partner. Toxic as he was, I actually owe billionaire fuckboy a huge debt of gratitude. He helped me put a healthy dating plan into action. The rest is fuckboy history.

CHAPTER EIGHT

Healthy Dating in Action (After Abuse)

B efore I came out as gay, I dated Siobhan from *Succession* . . . . Let me explain.

It wasn't the actress from the show, but it was a woman whose family was just as powerful and wealthy as the Roy family in *Succession*. They had a private jet, enjoyed dinners with the president of the United States, and were swimming in money, fame, and influence. And I dated their daughter. It would be my last relationship with a woman. Honestly, this woman had a long list of issues that had me reaching for the tissues.

I knew right away that she was . . . interesting. She was tender and sweet, but when she drank alcohol, she would dissociate and talk to the walls. When I brought it up to her, she made it seem like it was a totally normal thing. So, what did I do? Moved in with her, of course! After three or four months! Red flag, what? Perfect storm of unhealed trauma, who? As an infamous meme says, "Where some see red flags, I see a carnival." Ah, intertwined dysfunction.

You're not going to believe this, but it did not go well when we lived together. Shocker! She would say things to me like, "My ex-boyfriend has a better body than you," and, "You're fucking worthless." She even called me by her ex-boyfriend's name, like, multiple times, for the duration of our relationship. Did I leave when I saw all of these red flags?

Girl, no. I was looking for the cotton candy and another barf-inducing ride. Step right up!

I was like twenty-one or twenty-two years old and had a mountain of my own unresolved trauma. I was all . . . the fuck . . . in. And it was beyond toxic. She would wake me up at four in the morning not just vacuuming but ramming the vacuum into the bedroom door. She had me drive by her ex-boyfriend's house, abused drugs and alcohol uncontrollably, and while we were living together, she checked in to the most expensive rehab in the country.

Caught in the storm of my own mental health issues, I was ill-equipped to deal with this level of clinical turmoil.

I had been gaslit so thoroughly over the course of our relationship, I used to keep a mini journal in the notes app on my phone titled "Am I Being Treated Poorly?" Quick tip: if you have to keep a log like this, you are being treated poorly. But she was my first relationship, and I was head over heels for her. I turned myself inside out for four years desperately trying to make it work.

When we had an abortion, things really went downhill. She blamed me for killing her child. I later found out her mom said, "It's a good thing you got an abortion with Ryan."

While she was in rehab, she called to tell me she had cheated on me with a fellow patient. Then she checked herself out early from the facility. Of course, she expected me to pick her up, and I did because

I was losing my grip on reality at that point. She broke up with me immediately after rehab and got her own apartment, which was a relief, because I couldn't afford to move at that time. But she stayed at our apartment, even though she had a place of her own. I felt like a hostage in my own home. She was verbally abusing me one minute and having random guys pick her up from our place the next. She even turned her incredibly powerful family against me. Finally, I found a way to escape and move into my own place.

Within three months we were back together. She'd blamed me for everything. I couldn't understand why she hated me so much and was looking for a way to work on our relationship. Meanwhile, she was hallucinating that spiders were coming out of her skin. I tried to get her help, calling her mom to say I thought her daughter should be admitted to a psychiatric hospital. Her mom said, "Don't you dare." It seemed her family was more worried about the optics of her psychotic episode than they were about helping their daughter. I felt completely powerless.

I can honestly say this was the lowest point in my life. And you've read this book, you know that's saying *a lot*. Eventually, after a long string of casualties, including my self-esteem, her sanity, my sanity, her dignity, my dignity, our potential child, my demolished reputation with her family, we ended it for good. Actually, one day I woke up and she was just . . . gone. I didn't hear from her again after that.

I was suicidal. It took ages to recover from that relationship. I hear she's married now and seems happy, which makes me happy for her. I wish her well, I just wish her well—just from afar . . . where the vacuum, her insults, and the ghosts of her rehab boyfriends past can't reach me.

Here's what I learned from that relationship. If there is an imbalance in the power dynamic, be cautious. I was young, naive, and sadly lacking in the private jet department. She had everything, including a family that pampered and enabled her. I didn't stand a chance. One thing I wish I'd done is maintain my agency in that relationship. And I wish I'd seen all the red flags.

Red Flags to Look For When Dating

- Asking to move in together too soon. I don't think this can be overstated: anytime someone in a new relationship is pushing for things to move too fast, it's a giant red flag. It means they don't trust themselves enough to allow the relationship to run its natural course, and they want something locked down because they can't hold in their bad behaviors for too long.

- Family enmeshment. If your romantic interest's family is too involved in their life, that's a sign to run for the hills, especially if that family is in control of the person's finances and major life decisions.

- Brutal "honesty." If you're hearing, "I told you I was (fill in the blank) so you shouldn't be upset by it," they're using the warning of their shitty behavior to absolve them from their shitty behavior. If I said I was going to punch you in the face and then I punched you in the face and blamed you for getting upset, it would still be physical violence and would not be okay.

- Unchecked mental illness or addiction. Listen, I'm not one to judge anyone else over their mental health or addiction struggles. I certainly have my own. But if someone is in the storm of their struggle, they are going to take you into that storm with them. And listen, you don't have to go, even if you feel a strong sense of loyalty to them.

- Feeling like you have to fix someone. If you feel an undeniable urge to fix or change other people, this red flag sits squarely on your shoulders. This is a big indicator that you're in a codependent relationship. Fixers will always find someone who needs to be fixed. Maybe it's from a desire to repair old relationship wounds from the past that we were powerless to change at the time. Maybe it's a false sense of control. Maybe we are just so desperate to be loved, we will try to be the hero when we are the ones who need saving. Take off your cape, gorgeous. And focus on the parts of you that need to be fixed.

Even if your partner isn't openly displaying red flags in the beginning of a relationship, those flags might show up later. It's important to watch for warning signs throughout the course of the relationship to be sure you're not being abused. Some are more obvious than others.

Who's Got the Power?

Power dynamic is a big one. While it's not fair to expect a strict and constant fifty-fifty contribution, it should be equitable as much as possible. Brené Brown said it brilliantly on the *Tim Ferriss Show*, when she said, "Everyone says marriage should be fifty-fifty. That's the biggest crock of bullshit I've ever heard. It's never fifty-fifty." Instead of expecting fifty-fifty, she and her husband quantify where they are each day, in terms of energy, kindness, patience, and investment. For instance, if her husband comes home and tells her that he's at a twenty, she knows she'll need to step up her energy, kindness, patience, and investment to an eighty that day. She'll cover him until he can replenish his resources. If they are both tapped out, for instance, Brené is only at a ten and her husband is at a twenty-five, it's time to have a talk. They know that anytime they have less than one hundred combined, they need to sit down and make a plan for how to be kind to each other while they get through that slump.

Both partners won't be able to sustain an equal fifty-fifty contribution through the course of a relationship. One may become injured or sick. There could be a death in the family that weighs a partner down in grief. A person could be disabled or working on healing their mental illness with good days and bad days. The point is, your partner should be there to pick up the slack when it's needed. But if one partner holds all the power, say because their family is loaded and they don't have to work, but they aren't contributing to the relationship, or worse, they're holding it over their partner's head as a way to justify treating them poorly, beware!

Warning Signs of an Abusive Partner

- The power dynamic is unbalanced and being used against you.

- You question your reality. Examples: You're asking yourself, "Did I really say/do what they claim I said/did? Because I don't remember saying/doing that." Or, "Am I being treated poorly? Is this *really* normal?"

- Cheating (obviously)

- Manipulation/gaslighting (see "You question your reality")

- You're not sure if you can trust this person to take care of you if you're ever vulnerable or sick.

> - You're in a cycle of love bombing, followed by abusive behavior (more on this at the end of the chapter).

If you subtract the noise, the false promises, the unrealistic hope, the trauma cycles, the infatuation, and urge to fix someone, what's left? Do you have a solid foundation with your partner? Or are you standing in a pile of trauma rubble? It can be hard to let go of someone in whom you've invested so much time, energy, and heart. But be honest and ask yourself whether it would be hard to leave . . . or more devastating to stay.

Healthy Dating Versus Unhealthy Dating

Healthy dating in action starts with knowing what you want in a partner but also with recognizing red flags and warning signs before the relationship progresses. Just like healthy eating, you want to avoid toxic ingredients and foods that make you feel like shit. You also want to make sure you're getting nourishment and that the meal is delicious. Toxic ingredients like love bombing, moving too fast, family enmeshment, brutal "honesty," unchecked mental illness or addiction, lying, cheating, ghosting, gaslighting, and any generalized shitty behavior are going to make you sick. But a delicious date that tickles your taste buds while filling your body with love, ease, passion, happiness, and comfort, now that's a healthy five-course meal that I could eat every day.

If you want to date healthy, here are some examples of healthy versus unhealthy choices. Trust me, I've been guilty of all the unhealthy ones on this list.

HEALTHY DATING VERSUS UNHEALTHY DATING

Ingredients for healthy dating	Unhealthy dating ingredients to avoid
Allows the relationship to progress naturally	Accelerates the relationship with dizzying speed
Genuine interest in each other/ authentic connection	Love bombing
Each person knows what they want in a partner	Lack of self-awareness and no clue what they want
Healthy boundaries	Boundary violations/ oversharing/fawning
Ends things respectfully if it's not working out	Ghosts you, reconnects, ghosts again, plays mind games
Takes the time to get to know you without projecting their fantasies on you	Starts planning for the future on the first date
Knows when to be vulnerable and when to give you space	Clingy, hovering, needy, behavior
Shows up for you	Disappearing acts that rival the most dazzling magician
Has done the work of healing their trauma/addictions	Their trauma oozes over everything, leaving a sludge of unhealed chaos
Healthy relationship with family/chosen family	Codependent and enmeshed with their family
Equity in the relationship and a balanced power dynamic	One person has all the power and holds it over the other.
Equal treatment of love, kindness, and respect	You keep a note in your phone titled "Am I being treated poorly?

Compassionate honesty	They're brutally "honest," which just means they think they have a license to say cruel things to you
They respect you enough to have hard conversations and end things if they develop feelings for someone else	If they have feelings for someone else, they string you along and then ghost you instead of telling you the truth
Investment in mutual happiness	They are a thief of joy and will rob you of all that is good within you if they can

If you want to enjoy a healthy dating life, the first step is to do your own work to be a stable and healthy partner. That might mean therapy, getting honest with yourself about your unhealthy behaviors, or getting into a recovery program if that's what you need. Then, and only then, will you be able to find the person of your dreams, and be the person of someone else's dreams.

The Love Bomber

We both had shitty fathers. That's how we bonded after matching on a dating app. I called it trauma bonding, though I know that term has another meaning (when you bond with someone who abuses you and then love bombs you to get you back, trapping you in an addictive cycle, also appropriate for this story). We matched on a Tuesday, and he wanted to go out that Thursday. My birthday was Saturday, so I thought this would be a fabulous way to kick off my birthday weekend.

The connection was even stronger in person. We both worked in music, and it was refreshing to talk shop with someone who could relate. He was aggressively into me, which I found a little odd.

"I've never met anyone like you. You are the real deal. You're amazing and I'm having the best time with you."

It was a bit over the top but harmless enough, so I thought. We shared a ride home and he insisted on taking me out for my birthday that Sunday. I thought it was kind of weird. We'd known each other only for less than a week, and he wanted to take me out on my birthday? I ignored my intuition and said yes.

The following day was Friday, and I woke up to a text from him saying what a great time he had with me the night before. I wrote back that I did too and looked forward to our date on Sunday. Then, at 7:00 p.m., he FaceTimed me. In today's world, FaceTiming someone you just met without asking first is equivalent to showing up at their house unannounced. Still, I answered, and he said he just wanted to see how I was doing.

Aw, how sweet, I thought. Then, he called me again at 11:00 p.m. to tell me happy birthday (my birthday was the next day) and that he'd talk to me tomorrow.

"Sounds good," I said.

Then, at midnight, he FaceTimed me again, this time to sing "Happy Birthday." So this guy who I'd just met had just contacted me four times in one day. Is that weird? Nah. I shrugged it off, thinking he just really likes me!

The next day was my birthday, and I heard from him zero times, yet I could see that he was watching my Instagram stories. I texted him at around 4:00 p.m. to tell him I couldn't wait to see him and that I'd made a dinner reservation for our date the following day. No response. In fact, I didn't hear from him until the next day, three hours before our date.

"You're going to kill me," although it was a text, I could almost hear the coy, melodic tone in his voice. "A work thing came up and I can't meet for our date."

I was fucking pissed. He ditched me on my birthday? What the fuck? You'd think I would cut my losses at this point and be done. But naive baby Ryan still had some learning to do. "Yeah, sure, whatever. Let's meet Wednesday instead," I typed.

I didn't hear from him again until Thursday.

"How are you?" he texted, pretending he hadn't flaked on me twice just a few days before.

I was fucking confused! He'd given me countless compliments at dinner, contacted me four times in one day, sang to me on my birthday at the stroke of midnight, then he totally disappeared for a few days, canceled plans, made plans, and flaked on those plans again. Was he still into me? I was looking for answers, so I texted, "I'm headed to Vegas. Wanna come?"

I never heard from him again.

A few weeks later, I saw a picture on his social media of him with his new boyfriend. Then it hit me. He must've met this guy around the same time as he met me. Somewhere between our first date and second date, he'd formed a connection with this new guy. If he had just told me that he was talking to this other guy and things evolved quickly, I would have respected that. Instead, he left me in the spin cycle. One minute, I was the most amazing thing in the world and the next minute, he was ghosting me on my birthday. Now that I've matured in the dating world, I know that love bombing is the ultimate red flag, and I probably dodged a major bullet with this guy. At best, he was being dishonest and overdoing it with the adoration and affection. At worst, he was love bombing to cover up some major issues or even abusive tendencies. At the end of the day, he proved himself to be unreliable and not the one for me.

Healthy Dating Recipe

This exercise takes the compatibility scale a bit further and gets more specific.

Write a dating recipe for all the healthy ingredients you want in your relationship.

- Include the things from your nonnegotiables list and add all the healthy traits you want to see in a partner, that is, good communicator, likes nature, good sense of humor, and so on.

- Add ingredients for the kind of partner you want to be. Notice the places where what you wrote doesn't align with your current dating behaviors and who you are based on your actions. Those are the places that need healing and reflection.

- Get creative! What kinds of things do you want to do with your partner? Hiking? Swing dancing? Community gardening? Painting/art class? (Hint: your favorite activity spots may be the best place to find your potential partner.)

- Cut out the things that give you a stomachache or heartburn. Do you want your relationship to be infidelity free? Low on control and manipulation? Nonsmoker? Sober?

- Do the work to *be* the partner you want to attract in your life based on this recipe.

FUCKBOY LESSON *Number Eight*

In a sea of red flags, you can either sink or swim. Grab your life vest and get the hell out of there, honey.

After swimming in a sea of red flags for so long, I started to wonder, *If a healthy dating situation were ever to come along, would I even recognize it? What will I do if I meet someone worthy of my open heart?* Just as we learned to practice happiness, we must also practice conscious dating. We must put together our own recipe of what healthy dating looks like. Even if we are not interested in a full meal, such as a long-term relationship. It's okay to be a grazer if that's where you are in the moment.

Healthy dating doesn't have to have only a long-term relationship or marriage as the goal. For some, healthy dating means having fun with many different dates in a respectful way that honors you and the other people involved. That's what's so great about modern dating. We get to be the chefs, putting in the ingredients that make our individual taste buds sing. Some like spicy dating experiences, while others prefer comfort food. The point is to get to know yourself and your desires well enough to pursue fulfilling experiences in the dating world.

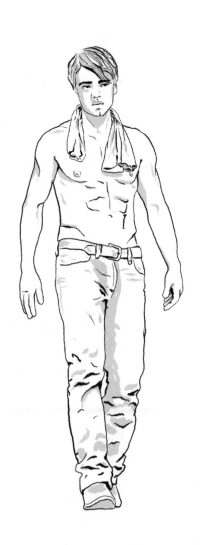

PART THREE

LOVE IS
~~A BATTLEFIELD~~
MY BIRTHRIGHT

CHAPTER NINE

I Fucking Met Him.
Now What?

I'd been flirting with this New York fuckboy for a while. He traveled to LA frequently, so we agreed to meet up the next time he was in town. It was close to Halloween, and I was thrilled to meet him in person. We had an instant connection and spent the whole weekend together. The first night we met up, I dragged him to the celebrity fuckboy's Halloween party (more about him in chapter eleven). It was your typical Hollywood party, with a lava rock firepit (even though it was 75 degrees outside), ironic anti-fame art on the walls, and the cast of the latest steamy Shonda Rhimes series eye-fucking one another near the mocktail bar. Blake was totally starstruck. My plan to impress him was going perfectly.

I told Blake I'd hooked up with the celebrity fuckboy before, just to make sure he knew how desirable I was. We weren't even invited. We crashed the party with my drag queen friend, Nova Kane, resplendent in her nine-inch platforms, flawless blue lace-front wig, and an attitude for the gods. Crashing the party was Nova Kane's way of getting back at the celebrity fuckboy for cheating on her friend with me. I was innocent and had no idea he was exclusively seeing someone else. He'd told me they had an open relationship at the time.

"That motherfucker. They were not in an open relationship. Fuck him, we're crashing his party, and I encourage you both to make a scene!"

And with that, we strutted into a glamorous but tasteful cliffside midcentury modern house to make shit real awkward for our cheating celebrity fuckboy. When we showed up, his assistant (who I'd also hooked up with) was caught by surprise.

"What are you doing here?" he said, wide-eyed.

I glanced over at Blake and did my best impression of James Dean. "You know *exactly* what we're doing here." I ran my fingers through my hair and made my way through a throng of TV stars, club DJs, and influencers. As soon as I got to the mocktail bar, I whipped around and made eye contact with Blake, nodding him over. Oh yeah, he was definitely into me.

"Where are you? Show yourself, motherfucker!" Nova bellowed, stomping through the party with as much subtlety as Beyoncé on stage during her Renaissance Tour.

Blake *loved* every minute of it. This was a first date for the record books and a perfect LA story.

He was in town only for a couple of weeks, so we had as much sex as we could. Sparks were flying, the butterflies in my stomach were on fire, and I couldn't wait to see him again. When he texted me on the Friday afternoon before Halloween weekend, I was ecstatic.

> Hey, what are you doing?

> About to get dinner with some friends. You?

I can't stop thinking about you. Let's meet up.

Great! I'd love to see you.

We made a plan, and on the night we were set to meet, I spent a full hour getting myself ready, but it was all in vain. He never showed up. No call. No text. He just didn't show. Ironically, this was the night I met the man who would become my boyfriend.

About a year later, I was working a modeling job in New York, and I bumped into Blake. We said a quick hello and I went about my day. That night, he texted me:

> "Hey, it was so good to see you. Want to come over for a drink?"

This was my Anne Hathaway in *The Devil Wears Prada* moment. In the film, she got everything she thought she wanted, but it wasn't working for her. So she threw her cell phone into a gorgeous fountain and strutted away through the Parisian streets in her Chanel pumps.

Here was this gorgeous guy texting me a year after he ghosted me, hoping to rekindle our situation-ship. Yet, to my surprise, it wasn't working for me anymore. First of all, I finally had a real boyfriend who I adored (still do). But that might not have stopped the earlier, unhealed version of me from indulging in sexy banter with Blake, or even meeting up with him.

Apparently the night Blake ghosted me, almost a year prior, had changed me forever (more on that later).

Ignoring Blake's call gave me a strange power. Suddenly, the roles were reversed, and he became the desperate one. He got to wonder why *I* wasn't calling *him*. This wasn't intentional like it used to be.

In the past, I had a roster when I was dating multiple men. My rule was to put the one I liked the most at the bottom, making a note to call them last because I didn't want to come off as desperate or annoying. I'd always say, "I gotta build that roster."

The Roster

A list to keep track of the people you're dating. It comes in handy when dating multiple people. The roster also serves as a helpful tool to rate your date, placing the ones you like the most at the bottom of the list so you can prevent yourself from coming off as desperate, needy, or annoying

Bottom of roster criteria

I've emotionally masturbated to them and couldn't stop thinking about them.

Top of roster criteria

They're there and I'm drunk or horny. I have a very low opinion of them and don't care if they think I'm desperate or drunk.

It may seem crude, but having a roster is critical for everyone who is trying not to get eaten alive in the modern dating jungle. Unfortunately, dating doesn't work out 99.9 percent of the time. If you get too attached too soon, you're not going to make it. Having a roster helps you create space for yourself as you get to know someone you like. Then, if you get ghosted, you won't be sitting at home crying into a tub of ice cream. I wouldn't ditch my roster until I'd been seeing someone for at least three months. That three months is like my probationary period. It's a realistic approach to dating that lowers the stakes and allows us the freedom to get to know each other without all the pressure. For me, the three-month mark is a place to pause and assess. In my experience, you can usually tell if the relationship is worth pursuing in the first ninety days. I would remove someone from my roster for one of two reasons:

1. They ghost.
2. It's past the three-month mark and there is no progression.

When I moved the dead weight off my roster, it left a space . . . a perfect space that was just my size. I was free to reflect on what I really wanted, who I wanted to be, and what I wouldn't tolerate anymore. I began to detox from all those juicy love chemicals that had been swirling around my brain, and I was able finally to get honest with myself.

Toxic Love Drugs

I would argue that all of the lusty, feel-good chemicals that course through our brains when we meet a fuckboy are just as potent as drugs. An article in Harvard's Science in the News highlighted the work of biological anthropologist Helen Fisher at Rutgers, which put different phases of relationships into three categories: lust, attraction, and attachment. When a person is experiencing lust, they are driven by elevated levels of testosterone and estrogen. If we find a person attractive, mood-boosting reward chemicals, like norepinephrine and serotonin, ignite like fireworks across our neurological pathways. If we make it past the fuckboy stage and into attachment, bonding chemicals like oxytocin and vasopressin bring us closer together with our love interest. We are chemically predisposed to get high on those brain chemicals, which make us seek connection with our crushes, even when it may not be good for us.

As it turns out, when we get hot and bothered, entire sections of our brains shut down. And surprise, surprise—it's primarily the ones we need in order to identify fuckboys. The areas in our brain responsible for critical thinking, rational behavior, and self-awareness are subdued when we meet a hot fuckboy. In other words, our lust and attraction chemicals are throwing a party in our minds that is so loud we can't hear the voice of reason telling us we're going to regret it all in the morning. These addictive chemicals were wreaking havoc on my nervous system and creating a never-ending cycle of chaos and despair. Although there were a few funny stories peppered throughout, it always ended the next day with shame and regret.

The thing about running through a constant storm of chaos is you never have time to stop and take a look at yourself. I was too busy, too excited, too steeped in drama to notice how much I was harming myself in these bad situations with people who didn't give a shit about me. My addiction to chaos kept me chasing the next high, the next guy, desperate for a fresh hit of those delectable brain chemicals.

Whenever I'd meet a new train wreck of a fuckboy, my brain would be flooded. When we feel that first spark of attraction our human brain starts producing dopamine, which makes us feel oh so good (they don't call it the feel-good chemical for nothing). Dopamine helps us with our motivation, movement, focus, and even has a part in breast milk production and, as an added bonus, creates feelings of bliss, euphoria, and desire. Ever wonder why we miss the parade of red flags about someone when we think they're hot and into us? It's science, honey.

When that dopamine hits, it shuts down our amygdala, the part of our brain responsible for fear, anger, and sadness. So we're not afraid of being ghosted, we giggle at the jokes they make at our expense, and we jump with glee when they text after ignoring us for a week. Dopamine and adrenaline together shut down the logic and reason parts of our brains, causing us to make rash decisions that could be bad for us.

When the adrenaline starts pumping, our hearts race, and we stay up all night thinking about the potential of the relationship. With heightened energy levels and excitement, we feel like we're on top of the world!

Oxytocin comes in and makes us bond with our new love interest. It makes us bond through touch, sex, and cuddling. It's the chemical released when you orgasm or when a mother breastfeeds her baby. It's nature's way of ensuring we don't have a bunch of feral babies crawling around the streets because their mothers didn't bond with them. With a new love interest, oxytocin makes us interested in getting to know our new potential mate. It inspires us to make long-term plans, pick out wallpaper, and introduce them to our parents.

These chemicals in our brains are the same ones that get hijacked by narcotics, gambling, and alcohol. According to Fisher, when we're at the height of our love-chemical secretion, we crave the other person the way an addict craves their drug of choice. It makes us willing to do crazy, ridiculous, unwise things. In some cases, we can become obsessive, and our realities can become distorted. This is what makes love addiction possible.

Love addiction is just as powerful as drug addiction. It actually ruins lives. According to love addiction psychologist Suzanne Philips, love addicts will obsess over connection, approval, and even their made-up fantasies about the other person. Even if there are moments of real connection, they can't possibly last under these conditions. Those moments become like a temporary high, keeping feelings of depression, fear of abandonment, and insecurities at bay. This turns the relationship into a whirlwind of euphoria, depression, and eventually, self-sabotage (which we'll cover in the next chapter). The only way to get out of this cycle is to deal with the pain underneath that all of those chemicals did such a good job of numbing.

When my love chemicals ran out, I was forced to deal with the truth, which was I didn't like myself very much. Every time I betrayed myself and did something that made me feel uncomfortable with a date, every time I stayed in a bad situation when I should have protected myself and left, every time I answered the phone call from a guy who'd treated me like trash, I was ghosting . . . myself.

I realized I needed to ditch my entire roster of fuckboys and replace it with one name: Ryan.

Am I Bored?

One great thing about my chaos addiction is that it makes me the life of the party. I'm all about spontaneity, whether that's an impromptu trip to Vegas or finding the best parties at a moment's notice. I'm the guy who knows how to have a good time. Let's be honest: sometimes a bit of unpredictability and chaos can be fun.

As I got healthier, I realized I needed to set boundaries with myself and others to stay healthy and happy. One tool I use to help me resist my pull toward chaos is meditation and mindfulness. When I'm about to make a decision that may not be in my best interest, I pause and ask myself, "Ryan, what will be the outcome in this situation?" I play the tape in my mind, and it usually goes something like this:

Me: Ryan, if you agree to meet this guy for a drink what will happen?

Also me: I'll start emotionally masturbating and do anything he says.

Me: And then what will happen?

Also me: I'll find myself riding shotgun in his shitty Honda that smells like weed.

Me: And where will that lead you?

Also me: Being fucked by a selfish hobbit. Or getting screamed at by their wife or with a crystal stuck in my ass or with self-tanner stains on my palms . . .

Me: You sure you want to go through all of that again?

Also me: No I do not, you clever, handsome bitch.

With this method, nine times out of ten I am able to make a choice that doesn't poison my well-being. Patience and engagement with this process helps me to identify, recognize, and reevaluate my triggers. Removing myself from the constant cycle of chaos and despair allowed me to begin to appreciate, love, and respect my life. It took me a long time to get there, but I've built a life that makes me happy. All that to say, there are times when I find myself questioning, am I bored? Usually, when I feel boredom, it's a sign that I'm craving that familiar chaos rush, which is my cue to look inward, remove myself from triggers if possible, or engage in my mindfulness practices. The irony is the moment I built a strong relationship with myself was the moment I was finally ready for a real relationship with someone else.

Thor

When I met him, I was dressed as a disco ball. I'd just left a friend's '70s Halloween party. There I was, in the heart of Boys Town, or the Gayborhood, as we affectionately call West Hollywood, stuffing myself into an Uber as gracefully as possible. Suddenly, the door on the other side opened and a guy dressed as Thor got into my Uber.

"Sir," I said with as much authority as a ball of tiny mirrors can have, "This is my Uber."

"No, it's not," he slurred. "It's mine . . . Oh, you're really cute!"

I was in my new era of no chaos, so I did my best to ignore him. But he kept asking me for my number. I finally agreed and gave him my business card. He texted me that night, but I ignored it and never responded.

A couple of weeks went by, and I was prepping for my big date with Blake. The fucker ghosted me, and although I was devastated in the moment, it turns out it was the greatest gift he could've given me. I picked myself up, dusted off my bruised ego, and set out into the West Hollywood night.

"Ryan!" I heard in a crowded nightclub later that night. "How are you?"

I turned around and saw Thor (without his superhero costume) standing in front of me. But I honestly had no clue who he was.

"We met last week. You tried to steal my Uber! Remember me? I was dressed as Thor."

In this moment, the effort that I'd been putting into my healing paid off. I had a moment of clarity—and I was able to see that there was something different about this guy. He seemed genuine, interested, and honest. That night, I found myself standing before two roads diverged in a Fuckboy Forest. One road was well worn and filled with ghosts, lies, dignity pitfalls, scary queens, thirst traps, and the quicksand of shame and loneliness. The other road was a mystery. It was quiet and had way less drama. All I had to do was take the first step into this unknown land of stable relationships. I had no idea what I was in for, but I was curious enough to consider this new road. A road that could potentially lead to the love of my life.

I wasn't responsive to Thor at first, but he was quite persistent. I finally took his call, and we started talking on the phone. It took a bit, but I finally asked him out on a date . . . then almost canceled that date. I had a perfect excuse; it was my uncle's seventieth birthday, and the whole family was meeting for dinner. My wisdom and healing prevailed, and I decided to reschedule instead of canceling. When we finally met, we had more fun than I'd imagined. Thor was a bit younger than I was and rather new to the gay dating scene. He'd just come out a couple of years earlier, which was good since one of my deal-breakers is someone who's still in the closet.

We were still seeing each other when I got COVID. This would have been the perfect opportunity for him to ghost me, but he didn't. He called me every day to see how I was feeling. Those daily phone calls showed me that he clearly cared about me. The chaos butterflies in my stomach were replaced by something deeper (hey, oxytocin), a more stable, sturdy, reliable feeling. We were building a relationship foundation.

The moment of truth was upon us. It was time to bring out my compatibility scale (cue epic movie music). I pulled out my list of criteria, clicked my pen in slow motion, and started rating. This was it. All of my dating mishaps, my journeys down to dirty rock bottom, my countless therapy sessions and relentless soul searching had brought me to this point. How would he rate according to the criteria of things that are the most important to me? Would he be a mediocre 3 or below? Or would he be a fucking fantastic 4 or higher?

To my surprise, every time I rated Thor according to my dating scale, he scored a 4 or above for each category:

- **Family values:** He loves and respects his family and makes them a priority.
- **Solid career:** He works as a nurse and finds it fulfilling.
- **Sense of humor:** We laughed together constantly.
- **Honesty:** He has always been genuine. He never tried to impress me with elaborate lies or grandiose behavior. I love how authentic he is.
- **How he made me feel (even when I had COVID):** I felt safe with him. He's one of the most stable people I've ever been with. He's never put me down or made me wonder if he's about to ghost me.

As I'm writing this book, my relationship with Thor is still going strong. We've been together for two years, and I'm learning to temper my addiction to chaos, which can sometimes present as "passion." Most dictionary definitions state that passion is a wild and uncontrollable feeling of lust, obsession, or anger. As a recovering chaos junkie, I knew I wanted to stay away from any wild, uncontrollable feelings or circumstances.

When I dug into the history of romance, passion, love, and marriage, I realized my view of these concepts was shallow. According to medieval lore, knights, troubadours, poets, and storytellers believed in a kind of passion characterized by worshipful devotion. It was an intense pining and often unrequited love from afar (when the knights were in love with his liege's wife, for instance). Inevitably, there was heartfelt poetry, longing, and devastating heartbreak when their love was out of reach. Has the meaning of passion changed with the times? What are the rules of passion now that human relationships have evolved? Well, it depends on your perception of relationships.

In psychology, passion is an indicator for a satisfying relationship but only when balanced with other key relationship factors. According to psychologist Robert Sternberg, who wrote about passion in 1986, passion refers to a longing or desire to be with someone, whether that's a romantic partner or the bond between parent and child. When it comes to love, Sternberg theorized that it's based on a balance of three things: intimacy, commitment, and passion. Intimacy, for me, is letting someone into your weird little world and allowing them to see the vulnerable parts of yourself that are reserved for one or a select few. Commitment is about showing up for someone consistently, remaining faithful, and staying through difficult times, rather than abandoning the relationship. Sexual passion can be indicative of a satisfying relationship. But too much intense passion can be dangerous and doesn't always lead to intimacy and commitment. That's why we need the balance of all three.

When it comes to love and marriage, the original reason people tied the knot could not be less romantic or passionate. The first evidence of marriage was in Mesopotamia more than four thousand years ago and served as a way for royalty to consolidate their power. Later, the church got involved and proclaimed it to be a holy union between man and wife, but before then there was a ton of polygamy happening everywhere. Marriage eventually became a way to make women subordinate to men, by exchanging them from father to husband like property and making them dependent on a spouse for their survival. (Uh, hello! A woman couldn't even get a credit card without her husband's approval until the 1970s!) In today's society, marriage is mostly about love and includes members of the LGBTQ community, but that doesn't make it any less complicated.

Set Boundaries ... with Yourself

It's time to bring awareness to your tendencies, whether it's self-sabotage, a pull toward chaos (like me), comparison, rumination, self-loathing, or whatever it is. Now, these tendencies can be sneaky little devils. They lurk in the shadows, just waiting for their opportunity to put a bag over our heads (or hearts) and keep us stuck in darkness. So in the moments when you're not at the mercy of these tendencies, it's important to plan for how to deal with them before they sneak up on you.

1. Write down your unhealthy tendencies. Don't be shy. Nobody is going to see this list but you.

2. For each tendency, create a plan for how to protect yourself or prevent yourself from getting swallowed up by it—or divert yourself before going on the path (see my conversation with myself). For example, if you're tempted to go into your old patterns, you'll leave, call a friend, or decline to take action for a certain period of time (say, twelve or twenty-four hours . . . long enough to give your nervous system time to recalibrate).

3. Write down what happens after you interrupt your tendency. Make a note of it every time you do something different. With enough repetition, your brain will start to rewire itself toward more healthy tendencies.

4. Give yourself grace if you fall back into an undesirable tendency. It happens. Don't get stuck in guilt, shame, and regret. Dust yourself off and move forward.

When you clear away your unhealthy tendencies, you'll open yourself up to new possibilities, like real love and deep passion, both for yourself and your partner.

—— FUCKBOY LESSON *Number Nine* ——

True passion is making someone (or yourself) a priority every day, not just when it's sexy.

What I discovered is that over time, the meaning of love and passion has changed for me. Now passion means someone who loves you enough to show up every day for you, even and especially on the hard days. Passion is predictable love that you can count on, not fleeting firecrackers of emotions that quickly burn out and smolder. Passion is waking up every day and actively choosing the person beside you. And it can also be hot sex and a longing to be together. We've been lied to about what true passion is. It's not the kind of passion depicted in movies, where lovers fight, then kiss, then get naked, then throw things at each other, then have sex, then fight, and so on. True passion is not about fucking and fighting each other; it's about uniting to fight the hardships of life together (okay, the fucking can still be a part of it). When we come to each other feeling content with ourselves, we have less desire to disrupt our relationships to serve an unhealed need for the chaos or instability we experienced in childhood. Then we can discover what true passion is for us.

I'm discovering that true passion, intimacy, and commitment with my boyfriend. This man is the person I would want by my side if I lost the person I trust the most in the world (my mom). If I hadn't done the work on myself, if I hadn't created that scale, I would have overlooked him. I'm still doing the work of recalibrating my system to recognize love . . . real love (thank you, Mary J.). With my partner, I'm discovering a love that doesn't require me to betray myself, turn myself inside out, guess the cruel game that's being played, or play out the cycle of abandonment that I've known since I was a fetus. This love allows for ease and space. The love we share is expansive, rather than restrictive.

So everything is fixed, right? Not quite. To my chaos-addicted brain, residing in a place of ease and peace can seem boring and unfamiliar. Left unaddressed, this boredom can lead to self-sabotage as a way to shake things up and create that oh-so-familiar and exciting chaos I'd been unconsciously seeking in one way or another since birth. For me, living in a healthy relationship means diligently pushing back against self-sabotage every day, so I don't ruin everything.

CHAPTER TEN

Sabotage Is a Bitch

I was mid–hand job in a dark bedroom when the door flung open and a woman yelled, "Get the fuck out of my house!" This was five years ago, long before my fuckboy awakening and before I met my long-term boyfriend.

While my hand was still on his dick, he looked at me and said, "You should probably go." The truth is, I should have left long before that embarrassing moment. The warning signs were everywhere.

I was with some friends when we met this guy at a bar. Without hesitation, he invited me back to "his place" and told me to bring my friend. "Let's have a party!" he cheered as he led us out of the bar. We thought we were going to a party at his house. Little did we know, we were about twenty hours early for the real party.

When we walked in, there were fifteen people sleeping on the floor in sleeping bags. Instead of seeing this as the first major red flag, I tried to rationalize this weird situation. *Okay, this is LA; rent is expensive,* I said to myself, ignoring the intuition that was flooding my system with warning bells. Never mind that by our age, we should have our rent situation figured out well enough to require fewer than fifteen roommates who sleep on the floor. *This is fine. This is fun. I am having fun!*

This guy led me into a bedroom, where he immediately racked up some lines of cocaine (my friend was in the bathroom hooking up with the other guy he invited). This was the second major red flag I completely ignored. I was not into snorting drugs in a random bedroom with a living room camping party happening just on the other side of the door. But did I get my friend and leave? Nope! I decided to hook up with this guy. Let the mid–hand job humiliation commence!

The weird part is *I* was the one who slinked away in shame that night. While it was embarrassing to get caught in the act, I think the real shame came from ignoring my intuition and those major red flags. I knew this was a mistake, but I self-sabotaged because I wanted this guy to like me. When it went horribly wrong, there was a little voice in the back of my mind that said, "You got what you deserved."

I ran into the Hand Job Fuckboy about six months later at a gay pride event. I reminded him that the last time we saw each other, I'd been kicked out of his house mid–hand job. I had to pick my jaw up off the ground when he said, "Oh yeah, my fiancée was asleep in the other room." Apparently, the reason all of those people were sleeping on the floor is because they were there for the guy's engagement party, which was planned for the following night. I was giving a hand job to the soon-to-be groom at the host of the engagement party's house.

"Oh, don't worry, we're in an open relationship," he said, as if that broad statement could wash away the entire weirdness of that night. "And we're married now. Want to make out?" Pass.

So you may be asking, "Ryan, why did you ignore all of those red flags in the first place?" Well, the answer to that question is layered.

When I was walking around in this body feeling unworthy, I accepted many unacceptable things just to feel accepted. I was willing to take unhealthy risks (a.k.a. self-sabotage) just to feel like I belonged in a society that sends constant messages telling people in larger bodies that we don't belong.

Unhealthy Risks Versus Healthy Risks

There's no way to avoid taking risks in life. If we never took any risks, we'd never leave the house, find new relationships, or meet any goals. But there's a difference between healthy risks and unhealthy risks.

The thing is, most people know they shouldn't be engaging in unhealthy risks. They know it's going to harm them eventually, one way or another, but they can't stop their risky behavior. Let's face it, unhealthy risks can be intoxicating (emphasis on the "toxic"). When I was in my fuckboy dating era, I took way too many unhealthy risks. It wasn't until much later, upon examination and deep soul-searching, that I understood why I was sabotaging myself in such toxic and scary ways.

My Reasons for Unhealthy Risk-Taking Behavior

- Low self-esteem
- Unhealthy body image
- Addiction to chaos
- Fear of missing out
- Superficial dating standards
- Fear of abandonment
- Running from the death-grip of loneliness
- Desperate to accept anything since I didn't know when the next guy was coming

EXAMPLES OF HEALTHY RISKS WHILE DATING VERSUS EXAMPLES OF UNHEALTHY RISKS WHILE DATING

Examples of healthy risks while dating	Examples of unhealthy risks while dating
Crossing a room to talk to a handsome stranger	Crossing the street at 2:00 a.m. to get in a car with a handsome, drunk stranger you just met
Finding a good match on a dating app based on your values and preferences	Matching on a dating app with a fuckboy who shares none of your values, but he's hot, so why not?
Going on a first date in a public place	Stepping over people in sleeping bags to give a guy a hand job in a dark room after he snorts rails of blow
Using protection and establishing boundaries and consent before having sex	Not asking them to use protection because you're intoxicated by lust and passion
Dating when you feel stable, happy, and healthy	Clinging to abusive people to ward off loneliness
Being your authentic self and hoping they like you for who you are	Being whatever you think they want and hoping you can trick them into liking you
Ending things if they mistreat or ghost you	Dropping everything when a guy who ghosted you three months ago texts you at 11:00 p.m. to hook up.
Telling your date after a few months that you'd like to take the relationship to the next level	Moving in together after three weeks of love bombing and partying
Prioritizing your safety and well-being, and those of the person you're dating	Ignoring your safety or well-being

From early childhood, I was conditioned to ignore my intuition and accept bad situations. My mother was amazing. She saw me being hurt by my father, by the bullies at school, by not feeling accepted by my peers and wanted to protect my tender heart. So she would often tell me to just "let it go" when bad things happened. She would say things like, "Oh, Ryan, don't worry about it. Just forget about it. Don't waste your time thinking about it. Don't let it ruin your day." Her advice came from the purest place of love and protection. She thought she was teaching me how to be resilient, and in some ways she was. But I was also learning to question whether my feelings were valid or if what was hurting me was no big deal.

This survival tactic, which was probably necessary during some of the rough times in my childhood that my mother couldn't protect me from, stayed with me well into adulthood. When I was in that abusive relationship with my ex-girlfriend, I found myself questioning if I was truly being treated poorly or if I should just get over it and let it go. This led to a dizzying dysregulation in my system because I felt I couldn't trust what I was feeling.

In addition to this outdated survival tactic my mother blessed me with, my father gaslit me all the time. When we finally reconnected in adulthood, his favorite line was "Oh, you're being so dramatic." We did a mutual therapy session once, and my father denied my painful experiences. He made me feel like I didn't really experience the traumatic events in my childhood. This gaslighting was so ingrained in us, my sister started doing it too. For the longest time, she kept telling me that my memories weren't true. It wasn't until recently that she came to me and admitted that those things were true and that she just didn't want to remember them.

It took a ton of hard work with my therapist to reacquaint myself with my true feelings. I needed reassurance that my feelings were valid. I learned that two things can be true. I am dramatic, and I now love that about myself. It's what makes me, *me*. And also, I have every right to react to the way I'd been treated in whatever way helped me process the trauma best. If that meant crying my eyes out, so be it. If that meant holding people accountable for hurting me, that's fine too. If I need to curl up in a ball and grieve, I allow myself that space to do so. I know my mother did her best, and I am grateful for her every day. But when survival tactics that we learned in childhood are no longer working for us, it's time to reevaluate them and create methods that work for us, ones that aren't dictated by anyone else's beliefs or perceptions.

Psychological Reasons People Engage in Unhealthy Risk-Taking Behavior

When people are taking dangerous or potentially harmful risks, they may not be aware of why they are doing those things. Psychologists say there are a few common reasons for dangerous risk-taking behavior:

- They get high on the thrill (for me it was the thrill of the uncertainty). Giving a stranger a hand job at a crowded slumber party may feel exhilarating . . . until you're getting kicked out of their engagement party.
- Peer pressure or social influence. All of us want to be liked, but some people take that urge a bit too far.
- Impulse control or mental illness. Any mental or behavioral disability that makes it hard to control impulses could cause someone to take unhealthy risks.
- Substance abuse. Not only is substance abuse a dangerous risky behavior, but it also leads to taking other unhealthy risks, as

our logic and inhibitions leave us the more alcohol or drugs we consume.

How to Avoid the Pitfalls of Risky Behavior

The pull to take harmful risks is still there for me sometimes. Part of my brain still believes that healthy risks are boring, while the rest of me knows the truth. Unhealthy risks usually end in very predictable ways, and after a while, there's nothing more uninteresting than being addicted to a fuckboy's uninspired laziness and selfishness. It's like doing the same thing over and over and expecting a different result. Now *that's* boring, and also the definition of insanity.

I'm happy to report that after many hard-learned lessons and, say it with me, hours of therapy, I've found a way to overcome the urge to follow through on those risky behaviors. It starts with one simple question: How is this decision going to affect me tomorrow? How about a week from now? A month? What about the rest of my life? There are some risky behaviors that have the potential to impact your life in a negative way, such as drunk driving or unprotected sex. If I take the time to look into the future, the thrill of it all sort of fizzles. I lose the rush of intoxicating uncertainty because I've made the consequences specific in my mind. If I go down this path, these are the highly likely outcomes. So I could hop in a car with this fuckboy and wind up hating myself tomorrow after something embarrassing or crazy happens or possibly find myself in the doctor's office with an STD or in jail for indecent exposure because he insisted I blow him in the car. Nah, I think I'll pass.

When I stopped wasting my time, energy, health, and self-esteem on unhealthy risks, it opened my life to new possibilities that began with healthy risks. Instead of obsessing over a fuckboy who hadn't called me in a week, I was out having fun with friends and meeting new people. With my new dating scale, I talked to guys I would have overlooked before. This led to interesting conversations with kind, decent people who shared my values. Soon, I realized the truth that inspired me to write this book in the first place. Fuckboys are boring. A life well lived can be exhilarating, breathtaking, and unpredictable in the best ways. My boyfriend makes me laugh in little unpredictable ways, he astonishes me with his kindness, and it's thrilling to take our relationship deeper and to discover the most intimate, vulnerable parts of him. Cutting out the dull noise of fuckboys also helped me to hear my own intuition better and with more clarity.

The Ex-Fucker

A good friend of mine was dating someone new, and I could see it all over his face. Anytime he talked about him, he bubbled over with excitement. I was happy for him and couldn't wait to meet his new date. But for some reason, he wouldn't send me a picture like he normally did in the past when he was dating someone new. I thought it was odd, but I didn't pay much attention to it.

My intuition started tingling when my friend asked me for advice on how to deal with their new love interest. It was oddly specific, like, "When you were with (let's call him Harry), how did you handle it when they didn't respond to your texts right away?"

That's weird, I thought. Still, I didn't say anything about my gut feeling. I asked him to send me a picture of the guy, but he still refused.

"The relationship is still new, and I don't want to jinx it," he said, avoiding eye contact with me. That just made the nagging feeling in my stomach worse.

I tried to be gracious with my extensive dating knowledge, pushing down all of my intuition's warnings. But after a while, my gut was screaming at me to voice my suspicions to my friend. My mind raced back to the time when I was with Harry and my friend kept commenting on how cute he was. Finally, I just asked him outright,

"Are you seeing my ex?"

"Yes," he admitted.

I couldn't believe it. My good friend was dating the guy who cheated on me with my neighbor and gave me scabies. Remember him? He's the guy from chapter four who sent me into my psychic hotline breakdown. My friend knew that I was far from over him because I confided in him about it all the time. I remember saying, "My ex randomly reached out to me the other day."

My friend looked a bit stunned and said, "Oh, really? What did he say?" He wasn't concerned for me; he was just trying to find out if my ex was looking to get back together with me. I was living in some *Real Housewives*–level betrayal, and I didn't even know it. Was there a camera in there with us? And did it capture my good side? I didn't even get the chance to have my moment in a tearful confessional to the camera. It was all bullshit, and my bullshit meter was broken.

Here I was, unknowingly giving my friend information and advice on how to have a successful relationship with my toxic ex who almost broke my soul. That hurt. I not only had to recover from a romantic breakup, but I also had to end things with my friend. He reached out to me a while later, but I couldn't get past what he'd done. I wished him well and never spoke to him again. It's one thing for a fuckboy to break your heart, but it's even worse when a friend does it.

My Intuition Is a Tired Old Queen

I imagine my intuition as this worn-out drag queen, standing on the porch, smoking cigarettes. I call her Stella Starlight. She used to waste her breath trying to warn me when she smelled trouble. First, she'd whisper. Then she'd raise her voice to get my attention. Eventually, she was jumping up and down, waving her wig above her head, and screaming, "Wake up, you fool!" It was exhausting. She broke too many nails and ruined too many wigs trying to stop my clueless ass from making yet another tragic mistake.

When she got tired of yelling, Stella gave up and just leaned back in her satin boudoir robe, taking long drags from a Virginia Slim and rolling her eyes as she watched me skip through the gay city streets with the latest fuckboy. She let the smoke out with a sigh, knowing the shame storm that was coming to her already weathered house. And when I came crawling back to cry on her faded Marabou slippers, she'd say, "Honey, I tried to tell you." It was always the same sad story. I'd wallow with my head in her lap, whining about my problems, and she'd listen as if she hadn't heard it a million times before. Stella was sick and tired of trying to look after me, especially when I wasn't listening. I was the reason she smoked three packs a day and didn't have time to get her nails done or shop for new wigs. With her eyes cast on the horizon longing for a better life, she'd run her chipped manicure through my hair and say, "I know, honey. I know."

If I was ever going to learn my lessons, I knew I needed to develop a meaningful relationship with Stella. Something remarkable happened when I started listening to her. I was finally able to break out of the constant loop of self-sabotage. I'm proud to say, that Stella is now down to half a pack a day and her wigs are gorgeous. All she has to do is clear her throat or tap her foot and my ears perk up. That queen deserves to be heard. She deserves respect. She tells me that I deserve respect too, and you know what? I have actually started to listen to her.

Connect with Your Intuition

How close are you with your inner knowing? Maybe your intuition isn't a drag queen like mine. Maybe yours is a beautiful goddess, a coach, or a guru. Take a moment, close your eyes, and imagine yourself in a nature setting, like the woods or the beach.

Once you've got your setting, invite your intuition to come and meet with you. As they approach, pay attention to the details of their appearance, the sound of their voice, and any objects they might be carrying.

Thank them for guiding you, even when you didn't listen. Tell them you plan to stay in deeper connection with them. Apologize, if it feels right. Then ask them if there is anything they want you to know. Listen and write down what they say. Ask them to give you a sign or symbol for when they are trying to get your attention. They might, for instance, place their hands on their abdomen to let you know that you'll feel it in your gut when something is off. Maybe they will show you a symbol, like a butterfly, that might pop into your head when you're about to do something that's not in your best interest. Spend time getting to know your intuition. Check in with them daily or weekly. You may be surprised to find they have a sense of humor, or you might feel calm in their presence. Forge a strong bond with your intuition and you'll notice that you'll have more wisdom, confidence, and a stronger sense of yourself.

FUCKBOY LESSON *Number Ten*

Self-sabotage always starts with ignoring your intuition.

When I look back on all the unhealthy choices I made in my fuckboy dating era, it's clear that Stella was sending me warning sign after warning sign. There were bells and whistles going off in my body, cautioning me that I was about to do something dangerous. Sometimes the warnings took the form of a knot in my stomach. Other times, it was a flood of fight or flight chemicals in my body. Stella did her best to stop me from putting myself in harm's way. Not only did I ignore those alarms, but I went running toward the danger. Full speed ahead. My low self-esteem was so strong, it drowned out all the warning signs. All Stella has ever wanted for me was to get home safe, heart intact and mind at peace. Silencing my intuition has always resulted in serious, sometimes hilarious, but mostly embarrassing consequences.

I encourage you to get in touch with your intuition. If it helps, give them a name and a persona. Have conversations with your intuition. Ask for its input and feedback. Having a good relationship with our intuition is the best way to prevent self-sabotage.

CHAPTER ELEVEN

Reciprocation Is Empowerment

I met Mickey at a sports bar in Florida. We were both in town visiting our parents and bored out of our minds. I wasn't attracted to Mickey, but I was horny and needed attention, so I thought, *Why not, let's see where this goes.* He offered to show me around town after dinner, so I got into his car. Suddenly, he pulled into a parking lot and whipped out his dick.

"Go down on me," he said with a straight face.

"Absolutely not," I said, proud of myself and all the therapy that got me to that point. He shrugged it off and dropped me back at my place. Later, he texted that he had a fun time and would love to see me again. I did not feel the same way at all. But I was in Florida, it was an easy hookup, and a guy has needs.

We'd made plans to have a full-day hook-up session in a hotel room. It was supposed to be an extravaganza of sex, room service, more sex, pillow talk, and lounging around in those soft white robes after our showers, glowing from postcoital bliss. But as soon as I got in his car when he picked me up, I remembered that this guy was five foot two, not cute at all, and had tried to get me to go down on him in a parking lot the last time we saw each other. *I'm so not into this*, I thought to myself as I smiled at him and he drove us to the hotel. Geez, how many drinks did I have last time? Oh, how quickly my dick (and alcohol) makes me forget these crucial details.

At this point, we were committed to the day. We'd already paid for the hotel room, and I was in his car, so how was I supposed to get out of this? By the time we arrived, I still had no ideas except to just go through with it. As we checked in, I tried to distract myself from my very loud thoughts saying, *Can we just leave? Is there a fire alarm I could pull to get out of this?*

No such luck.

In the room, we got right to it. I started going down on him, then he went down on me. Then we switched again, and he finished. I stood there, awkwardly for a bit, looking at him like, *Okay, my turn.*

"Oh, you must be under the assumption that I finish guys off. But I don't do that," he said, again with a straight face. What? I don't think I've ever angrily jacked off before, but as I finished myself off, I gave him the dirtiest look. Suddenly, our extravagant, all day sex fest turned into a one-sided thirty-five-minute disappointment. I could have saved the money and jerked off at home. Neither of us could wait to get out of that room. I should point out that while this doesn't happen frequently in gay sex, it does happen. It's happened to me several times, and before I had built up some self-confidence, I took it personally and as a reflection of me not being good enough. But in this situation, I saw the truth that he was the shitty person in this equation.

Mickey drove me home and as he dropped me off, he said, "Let's hang out again," without a shred of awareness.

"Sure," I said. But in my mind, I was saying, *There's no way in hell, you selfish hobbit.* I flashed him a fake smile and got out of the car. Later, I found out that he'd blocked me on all the social media apps. I didn't know what to make of that.

I couldn't understand it. This dude had nothing going for him (well, maybe his car) and had the audacity to block me? The interesting part is that I still took it personally. I couldn't help but wonder, *Am I really so bad that even a guy I wasn't into blocked me?* I'd come a long way, but I still hadn't found the peace of mind to let that one go.

Before therapy, I believed every guy was out of my league in one way or another. Later, after working with a therapist, I developed my self-esteem and swung too far in the other direction. I started operating on the assumption that I was better than everyone else. I suppose it's possible that Mickey picked up on that energy and it activated his inner selfish hobbit. In my mind, I was this six-foot-four daddy graciously blessing this unattractive creep with my time, and he had the nerve to reject me? It took some reflection, but after a while, I had three realizations from that experience:

1. If I'm not into someone, I shouldn't pursue the relationship or the hookup.
2. I'm not better than anybody and nobody's better than me.
3. Reciprocation is empowerment.

What Is Reciprocation?

We've already established that it's not possible for each person in a relationship to give exactly 50 percent at all times. Sometimes a partner can only give 20 percent while the other gives 80 percent. But problems arise when one partner is always giving the bare minimum while the other is giving more than their share of the love, care, pleasure, financial support, emotional labor, and responsibility. The *Cambridge Dictionary* defines *reciprocation* as "the act of feeling or behaving toward someone else in the same way they feel or behave toward you."[2] That means, if my partner needs emotional support, I do my best to meet that need, knowing that when it's my turn to need support, he will do the same for me.

Now, I'm not into bean counting or keeping score. There's a difference between reciprocation and transactional relationships. If I am doing nice things for my partner only because I expect something in return, that's transactional and not based in love and respect. That said, if I'm constantly there for my partner and he rarely shows up for me in the same way, we'd need to have a conversation. Reciprocation is about both people in a relationship feeling seen, heard, honored, and respected.

Reciprocation and Misogyny

Reciprocation is not just about sex, though the bedroom can be a good indicator of how your partner values and satisfies your needs in other areas of life. But let's talk about reciprocation in sex for a moment. According to a report published in *Archives of Sexual Behavior*, 95 percent of straight men say they usually or always have orgasms during sex, compared to 89 percent of gay men, 88 percent of bisexual men, 86 percent of lesbian women, 66 percent of bisexual women, and 65 percent of straight women. The travesty is, none of my straight female friends are surprised that they are dangling at the bottom of this orgasm statistic. While gay men do much better when it comes to getting off, there are still selfish lovers out there. But when we value ourselves enough to ask for reciprocation from our

---

2   *Cambridge Dictionary*, s.v. "reciprocation," accessed January 20, 2024, https://dictionary.cambridge.org/us/dictionary/english/reciprocation.

partners, either they will make more of an effort or show that they don't give a shit. If it's the latter, you know who they are and can be confident in your decision to leave the relationship (or refuse the next hookup with them). Life's too short to waste it on someone who doesn't give a shit about you and your needs.

Reciprocity in relationships isn't just about sex. It's about the balance of give and take with empathy and emotional caretaking, division of labor (making plans, household responsibilities if you live together, parenting, and so on), and even agreeing on what activities and shows you watch together. If your man insists on watching *Drag Race* all the time and you never get to watch *Bridgerton*, you either need to get two TVs or have a serious discussion about reciprocity.

I know from conversations with my straight women friends that there are so many tragically self-centered straight men. They don't understand anything but their own needs and their own biology. I have a good friend who once told me, "They're so clueless, I'm literally on Tinder while they're fucking me." No wonder women are losing interest in marrying straight men. There is a whole movement of women who'd rather live alone with their cats or other single women than deal with straight men's ineptitude. And I don't blame them. Our society is filled with men (both gay and straight) who don't reciprocate sexually, don't do emotional or domestic labor, and don't give back at all in relationships.

Many of these men believe they don't have to reciprocate because they think it's beneath them. I recently came across an article about DJ Khaled in which he said he doesn't go down on his partner because he believes there are "different rules for men." He thinks a woman should praise her man and treat him like a king. He added that a man should praise his queen, but he meant by saying things like, "You like the house you living in? You like all them clothes you getting?"

In his mind, he is entitled to oral sex because he makes more money and buys material things like housing and clothes. But she is not entitled to reciprocation of pleasure because he provides those material things. Granted, this interview was in 2015, and I hope for his wife's sake that he has examined this sexist double standard since he said that stupid shit out loud. But it seems that many straight men are defaulting back to archaic sexist beliefs rather than reciprocating the needs of their partners. Perhaps this is why our patriarchal society insists on devaluing the work of women, so they can place them in inferior positions when it comes to relationships and their personal power. If a woman can provide her own housing and clothing, she might have the audacity to demand equal treatment in her relationships.

The term *high-value male* comes to mind. There is this cesspool of misogynistic influencers claiming there are "high value" men that women should bow down to and deem superior. Honey, your balls stink too. Stop expecting women to have pristine vaginas, low body counts, and no desires other than to please you. What happens when you expect your partner to do all the caretaking with no reciprocation? The relationship changes to more of a parent/child dynamic. Women don't want to fuck someone they're mothering. And gay men don't want to fuck someone who doesn't care about their needs either.

Reciprocation: The Game Show

All of this got me thinking, what if we vetted our dates by asking them a series of rapid-fire questions on reciprocity before wasting our time with assholes who care only about themselves? It wouldn't be a Hollywood fuckboy story without at least one bad script, right?

RECIPROCATION
By Ryan Sheldon

INT. GAME SHOW SET—DAY

Two attractive men stand at podiums on a colorful and well-lit set of the game show "RECIPROCATION." Our host, the affable Grant McKenzie enters, a giant smile plastered across his artificially tanned face.

> GRANT
> Who's ready to play . . .

The studio audience shouts in unison.

> AUDIENCE
> Reciprocation!!!!

Wild applause . . .

> GRANT
> Our first contestant is a thirty-five-year-
> old lawyer who has never given
> anyone an orgasm and also, he can't
> operate a stove! Give it up for
> Briannnn Bradford!

The audience cheers wildly.

> GRANT (CONT'D)
> Contestant number two is an
> electrical engineer who always
> pays for dinner and thinks that
> should be enough, let's welcome
> Iannnn Schmidt!

The audience goes berserk.

> GRANT (CONT'D)
> Gents, get your buzzers in hand and
> let's . . .

> AUDIENCE
> PLAY! THE! GAME!!!

Wild applause!

> GRANT
> This is the rapid round fellas, and
> here we . . .

> AUDIENCE
> GO!

> GRANT
> Okay, after your date satisfied
> your wildest sexual fantasies, you:

Brian buzzes in.

> BRIAN
> Ask him to call you an Uber.

A buzzer that sounds like a disappointed sigh rings out.

> GRANT
> That is incorrect. Ian?
> Care to weigh in?

Ian keeps pushing his buzzer, trying to get it to make a beep.

> IAN
> Can you show me how to work this?
> Or can someone just push the button for me?
> Buttons aren't really my thing.

> GRANT
> We'll come back to you. Next question!
> Your partner just listened to
> you droning on about your boss for
> the last hour. Now it's time for you to:

Brian buzzes in.

> BRIAN
> Ask for a blow job.

The disappointed sigh sounds.

                    GRANT
                  Wrong again!

*Ian is pushing his buzzer with both of his thumbs and
jerking it around wildly.*

                     IAN
          Why do I have to push my own buzzer?
                 This is so unfair.

                    GRANT
          Ian, you don't have to push it that hard.
        That's, you're not even hitting the right spot.
                     Ian?

*Ian has thrown the buzzer to the ground and is stomping and
jumping on it.*

                     IAN
              Stupid! Fucking! Buzzer!

                    GRANT
          Ian . . . never mind. Final question!
                Your date says he wants to
              see a movie of his choice. What
                   should you do?

Brian buzzes in.

                    BRIAN
          Sulk and give him the silent treatment
              until I get my way and we go
            see the same Marvel movie we saw
                  last weekend.

Disappointed sigh sounds.

                    GRANT
          I'm sorry, your answer is not only wrong,
          but you are a disgrace to humanity, and
              I feel sorry for anyone who has
                 to spend time with you.

Ian is in full temper tantrum.

                    IAN
                  (crying)
        You know what, I'm out of here.
        I don't need this. I'm awesome
           and my thumbs are strong!

Ian stomps away from the podium, gets caught in the buzzer cable, and falls, bringing the podium crashing down on top of him.

                    IAN
                Mother, help!

                   GRANT
        And that's all the time we have.
         As usual, nobody wins when
             selfish fuckboys play:

                  AUDIENCE
              Reciprocation!!!

Brian stands there with his hand out, waiting for a prize as the audience applauds and the set goes dark. Ian is still wrestling with the podium.

                          The (Tragic) End

If only it were that easy to spot the ones who don't reciprocate. Instead, we have to waste time with pointless messages and then go on dates where they eat food off your plate and take you back to your place for an unsatisfying sexual experience.

A Quick Note About Codependency

If you're like me and a ton of other people who, as children, were traumatized into being codependent shadows of themselves, know that this is a safe space and I'm not judging you at all. So many of us have been brainwashed into believing that we are only lovable when we are of use to someone else, a.k.a. giving away all of our love, gifts, energy, sex, time, money, resources, and labor. But that's not how relationships are supposed to work. (Trust me, it was a surprise to me too!) My value is that I exist as a human being and I deserve to feel good, to feel cared for, to have an orgasm. So does my partner. So do you. If this is a struggle for you, Melody Beattie's book *Codependent No More* is a helpful resource to get you started.

Codependency can make us think we should accept less from our partners than we give. We may feel worthy only if we are overgiving, oversharing, and overworking ourselves to the point of exhaustion. Some codependents are so out of touch with their own needs, they don't even know what those needs are or how to ask for them to be fulfilled. For those working to heal that codependency, I recommend making a list of your needs. Write down more than just your survival needs. Include your specific needs regarding pleasure, joy, fulfillment, and peace. Then start fulfilling your own needs so you get used to how that feels. Once you start to feel the satisfaction of your needs being met, you'll be more inclined to ask others to meet your needs. And if you feel guilty about asking for your needs to be met, just know that real "high-value" partners enjoy meeting the needs of the people they love. So you are giving them an opportunity for fulfillment as well. True reciprocation makes both partners feel empowered.

Masculine and Feminine

There is a sort of yin and yang when it comes to reciprocation. Sometimes, I want to take charge with a more masculine type of energy. For instance, in my professional work, I tend to take a more masculine approach. But there are times when I want to enjoy my feminine side. I think this is a tricky balance. For me, as a gay man, I am constantly trying to balance my masculine and feminine energies. I define masculine as the side responsible for making plans, being structured, finding solutions, meeting deadlines, and being an initiator. My feminine energy is about creativity, nurturing relationships, beauty, intuition, and opening up to receive. In my relationship with my boyfriend, sometimes I want to be the initiator and plan maker, but other times, I want him to take that role. Then there are times when I need him to be nurturing and soft, a.k.a. more feminine. This is why open communication is so important when it comes to reciprocation. Our needs change on a day-to-day, sometimes moment-to-moment, basis. We need to stay in tune with one another.

Before anyone comes at me for assigning certain traits as feminine or masculine, I acknowledge that we've been conditioned to see women as the soft nurturers and caretakers while we see men as solution-minded initiators. But gender is fluid; we all have masculine and feminine energy to varying degrees. To discount it all as mere stereotypes would be to discount our ability to embrace the gifts and strengths across the spectrum of feminine/masculine. The butch/femme dynamic is a real thing in gay culture. Many of us have spent lifetimes learning to embrace our feminine nature in a masculine-dominant society where "men are men." Gay people have often been bullied for being too "girly" or too "mannish." Some have been assaulted for having feminine/masculine mannerisms and traits that go against the binary societal expectations of women and men. And in worst-case scenarios, we've even been killed for not being manly/womanly enough. These ideas of femininity versus masculinity were around long before I got here, and we don't yet have the luxury of dismissing the societal beliefs about what it is to be feminine or masculine. But I do have the power to embrace what works for me and balance the feminine/masculine energy that is present in all of nature.

Masculine or feminine, reciprocation can happen only if your partner is paying attention to your needs and your cues. If they are ignoring your cues, they're probably not giving you much pleasure, and may even be causing pain.

Warning Signs of a Nonreciprocator

To be honest, there were warning signs that the hobbit was going to be selfish long before we got into bed together. If I'd had someone alert me to these warning signs, I could have saved myself from that awkward experience.

But since I know them now, I'm sharing them to save another poor soul:

- Never asks your opinion on places to meet for dates
- Orders for you at a restaurant without asking you what you like
- Ignores you when you're talking to them or constantly interrupting you
- Late-night booty calls
- Invades your comfort zones (or makes fun of you when you're uncomfortable)
- Pressures you to do things you don't like
- Invades your boundaries (not asking for consent, calling when you've said you're busy)
- Laughs at your expense

Little Acts of Love

Now that I'm in a loving, committed, respectful relationship with my boyfriend, a.k.a. Thor, I can see how important reciprocation is and how special I feel when it happens. I've told you several tales of dates gone wrong. Now let me tell you about a love gone right.

First, let me say that the movies have lied to us. Grand, dramatic gestures, like the ones we see in romantic comedies, are overrated and fleeting. True reciprocation comes in the form of daily acts of love. Here's what I mean:

Every year for my mom's birthday and Mother's Day, my boyfriend makes it a priority to call her and makes a plan with me to get her gifts. He does this because he knows how important she is to me. This little act of love says, "She's important to you, so she is important to me."

He also does this for my sister on her birthday.

He cares for my dog, who is like my child to me. Our first Christmas together, after we'd only been dating for a few months, he got my dog a Christmas ornament, even though I'm Jewish. My dog doesn't recognize religion and was totally cool with it. He takes the dog out for walks and cares for him like he's his own.

I had given him a key to my apartment and had been out of town for a bit. When I got home, I was washing my face and saw a note on the bathroom mirror: "I'm glad you're home. I'm so excited to see you!" He leaves me notes all the time and I save them. It's a little thing that makes me feel loved in a big way.

When I was in Florida, visiting my mom, there was a knock at the door. It was a coffee delivery that my boyfriend had sent to us. It was exactly what we liked. He actually pays attention to what I like? That was a new one for me.

When I got a new job, we went out to dinner to celebrate. I had no idea that he'd called the restaurant ahead of time to ask them to do something special for me. When the dessert came out, they brought a tray with an assortment of treats, and on the plate, he had them write in chocolate, "Congratulations, Ryan! I'm so proud of you." He paid for the entire meal. I'd never experienced someone celebrate one of my wins in such a meaningful way before. And I do the same for him. We celebrate each other and are also there for each other during the hard times (like when I had COVID, and he checked on me every day).

These little acts of love make a big difference. But we also spend time learning each other's love languages, the concept made famous by Gary Chapman's book *The Five Love Languages: How to Express Heartfelt Commitment to Your Mate.*

My love language is words of affirmation. So my boyfriend makes an effort to pay me compliments and say loving things to me. He texts me every day with "good morning" texts and asks me about my day. His love languages are being touched and quality time. So I spend time cuddling him and holding his hand, giving him physical affection.

I'm not naturally a physically affectionate person, but since I know that's important to him, I make an effort to do that for him, so he feels loved by me.

Grand gestures are nice, but I prefer the little acts of love. They require more thought, effort, and consistency. To be honest, I think grand gestures are more for the giver's ego than the receiver. Give me the consistent, tender moments, thoughtful dinner surprises, birthday presents for my family members, and notes on the mirror. These little acts remind me every day that I matter to him, that I am loved, and that my needs are important to him. I love that we show up for each other every day in big and small ways. But it's in those daily details that I see just how much I mean to him, and he sees how much he means to me.

What's Your Love Language?

According to Gary Chapman, there are five love languages:

- Words of affirmation

- Quality time

- Acts of service

- Physical touch

- Receiving gifts

These are a great start, but I think there are more than five love languages. Maybe yours isn't on this list. That's okay. Write down the things that make you feel loved, and create your own list. If you are in a relationship, ask your partner about their list. Once you know each other's love languages, think of small acts of love you can do on a daily basis that will make your partner feel loved.

FUCKBOY LESSON *Number Eleven*

Look for the warning signs of a nonreciprocator way before you see them naked.

Whether you're in a gay or straight relationship, you deserve to have your needs considered and met. So many men out there find it totally acceptable to leave their partners unsatisfied. They also obligate their partners to participate in unsatisfying sex. But it doesn't have to be like that. It's important to watch your date for the warning signs mentioned previously and challenge them when they are ignoring your needs long before you get into bed with them. If they're not willing to listen to you when you're speaking, what makes you think they'll pay attention to what makes you orgasm or what makes you feel loved? Life is way too short to be with someone who doesn't reciprocate your emotional and physical needs. If only I could tell these fuckboys about the harm they've caused and continue to cause others. If only I could talk to my younger self with love and compassion as I navigated through the Kingdom of Fuckboys.

CHAPTER TWELVE

Love Feeds Self-Love

A n Open Letter to All the Fuckboys I've Loved Before:

In the story of my life, your chapters were once the most vivid. Through each of you, I learned about the vast spectrum of love—from its innocent beginnings to its most painful ends. I once allowed my innocence to be stolen and overshadowed by the shadows you cast. And while I bear responsibility for opening that door, my greatest regret is that I scolded myself for it for far too long.

You might believe that you left an indelible mark of sorrow on me, and for a while, that might have been true. There were moments I felt so crushed, so shattered, I believed I would never find the strength to love again. But, as time moved forward, love found its way back to me; a love far deeper, more sincere, and infinitely more profound than I had ever known with any of you.

The tears I shed, the nights I spent questioning my worth, and the weight of the betrayal—they were heavy, but they were not in vain. Every ounce of pain you inflicted became the foundation of the boundless love I've discovered now. It's a love that feels like the first rays of the morning sun after a stormy night—pure, warm, and healing.

Sometimes, you do cross my mind, not from a place of longing but of gratitude. I'm eternally thankful for the lessons I've learned and the strength I've gained. The love you offered, which I once mistook for genuine, was a distorted reflection of what true love should be. I once thought that was the love I deserved, but I now know that what you gave is something I wouldn't wish upon my worst enemy. While my spirit was broken and beautifully rebuilt, yours remained just broken.

In the aftermath of our time together, I felt fragments of myself scattered, lost amid chaos and confusion. Every day was a battle, and it took every fiber of my being to piece myself back together. Your words once held power over me. You labeled me a "good time," trying to reduce my worth. But today I stand tall in the knowledge that I am not just good for a moment; I am inherently good.

In the grand scheme of things, you all were mere stepping stones on my journey of self-discovery and self-love. You played your parts, steering me down a path that led to the most profound love affair of all—the one I have with myself.

To all the ones who suffered from my time as a fuckboy, I want you to know that I'm sorry for my actions. I assure you: it had nothing to do with you and everything to do with me. I was insecure and looking for love in unhealthy ways when what I

really needed was to be honest and loving to myself. I wasn't
ready to show up in the ways you may have needed, and for
that, I take responsibility. You deserve better and I hope you
find it.

So, to all the fuckboys I once loved, thank you. Thank you for
unknowingly guiding me toward the truest form of love. You may
have been chapters in my story, but I am the author, and I have
changed the narrative. I've emerged as a man who knows his
worth, understands the depth of genuine love, and cherishes
the magic within him. I wish the same for you.

Releasing with love,
Ryan

A Different Kind of Bottom Story

I've shared my rock bottom stories with you; now it's time for a different bottom story. As I mentioned before, I came out as gay later in
life. I was in my thirties and completely clueless. Since I had no idea
about the dangers of having sex with someone who doesn't care
about your needs, I lost my virginity with a man in a pretty cruel way.

And now it's something I've had to live with every day since.

I was new to gay sex at the time, especially bottoming. I'd never
been a bottom before and had no idea what to expect, how to pre-
pare, or how to protect myself. I trusted the guy I was with to take
care of me and protect me. Instead, he gave me a serious injury.

He didn't warm me up or do what he should have done to ensure
this would be a safe and pleasurable experience for both of us. He
knew what needed to be done, he just didn't care to do it. I, however,
as someone who had never done that before, had no clue what to do.
It was exciting at first, but it quickly turned painful. I did my best to
hide the pain because it was my first time, and I was embarrassed

and ashamed. It didn't last very long because I said I needed to stop. He had just let it rip and literally ripped me. There was blood everywhere, and he had the nerve to be grossed out! Luckily, he was wearing a condom, but he was still horrified. I was in shock and asking him, "Is this supposed to happen?"

His reply? "First times suck."

Six years later, I'm still dealing with issues from that injury. It can be hard for gay men to find doctors who know how to treat them, specifically when it comes to anal sex. In many towns, proper health care for gay men isn't accessible due to shame and lack of knowledgeable doctors. With the overturn of Roe v. Wade, women are experiencing a similar lack of care for their reproductive health and safety. Even our medical system is disproportionately based on the needs and beliefs of cisgender straight men.

As part of my recovery from the injury that selfish jerk gave me, I have to get Botox injections and go to pelvic floor therapy once a week. Having a partner who doesn't care about your needs or safety can have life-altering consequences. To be honest, there were warning signs that he wasn't going to reciprocate. He didn't give a fuck about me and was only concerned with his own experience of pleasure. Not only did he ruin that experience but many subsequent experiences after he was long gone.

Sex can be an extremely painful experience for me at times because of this injury. Now that I have a loving and caring partner who does reciprocate, I can't have anal sex with him as much as I would like. One encounter with one selfish fuckboy has affected my sex life for years. Every time I go to the doctor, I think about sending him my medical bills because I've spent tens of thousands of dollars repairing the injury his selfishness caused. Looking back, I should have pressed charges against him. He caused a life-altering injury that has lasted for years. Be careful with the selfish ones.

Exorcising Ghosts of Fuckboy Past

The fuckboys on my Wall of Shame have haunted me for years. Each of them took possession of my body and my life, some for a short time, some for way longer than I care to admit. Some left me with permanent injuries. But all of them carried a lesson that, when I took the time to understand, allowed me to evolve with a love for myself and a sense of peace that no fuckboy could shake. I was like a sinking boat with gaping holes in the sides from the cannonballs of child-hood trauma. Each fuckboy entered my life through a hole in my self-worth that I needed to heal so I could float again. They showed me what was damaged, bringing my attention to the parts of me that needed repair. As I methodically patched those holes, and my head emerged from the water, I could finally breathe and see the vast ocean of possibility in front of me. That gave me the courage to make those fuckboy ghosts walk the plank and never return to my voyage again.

Is anyone else getting sexy pirate vibes from this analogy? Okay, focus Ryan.

Recently, my boyfriend asked me if I would trade all these fuck-boy experiences if it meant I wouldn't have had all the heartbreak. I know it's popular for people to say they wouldn't change a thing, not even the painful things, because everything they went through helped them become the person they are today. I disagree. The truth is, I would happily trade all the heartbreak because that kind of pain changes you. I have to work every day to heal from the pain of my past. While I found a love that is more profound than ever, both for myself and for my boyfriend, I can't help but wonder how the pain of my past colors that love. Perhaps I wouldn't have as much grati-tude for the love I've found if I hadn't been exposed to the darker side of dating. Maybe I would've taken it for granted. I think both things can be true. I had to pull myself out of the online dating fuckboy hellscape to get to a place of true love and acceptance. But I want to do everything I can to make sure someone else doesn't have to go through that suffering.

The truth is, I have every right to be pissed off at these fuckboys for using me, lying to me, betraying me, ghosting me, and making me lose countless hours of sleep, not to mention my health and sanity. But that anger only invites these ghosts to keep haunting me. A bizarre and wonderful thing happened when I forgave and found love for myself. I was able to forgive all the fuckboys who'd hurt me before, including the OG, my dad. When we feel powerless, we wish harm on those who have harmed us. But when we are fully in our own power, we wish them the same peace and wisdom we've found for ourselves.

Through that peace, I've been able to exorcise the fuckboy ghosts of my past and move forward to the land of the living. While I love my life with my boyfriend, I am truly my best partner. There is no need for me to betray myself for one night of awkward, uncomfortable, sometimes painful sex. I've become the loyal man I needed in my life. The irony is, when I stopped needing that love and loyalty from the outside, the perfect partner showed up with his Thor hammer and rocked my disco world.

Fuckboy Lessons

If you've made it this far in the book, that means we've been through a lot together. My hope is that you can take the lessons I've learned and create value out of them. Or at least that my crazy dating stories made you chuckle and gave you good material for gossip on margarita night with your friends. I love a good recap, so I'm putting all the fuckboy lessons here for you in one place:

1. If they see you only as parts, whether in person or on a screen, you'll never be a whole human being to them.
2. If you're going to be a fuckboy, at least try to be a good fuckboy so you don't end up on someone's wall of shame.
3. Never take a fuckboy at face value (no matter how gorgeous that face is). Pay attention to what they do over what they say.
4. Sometimes our own mind lies to us just as much as (or more than) fuckboys do. It might make you believe the world is ending or that you're worthless when it's not and you're not. Ask yourself if what you're thinking is really true. Fuckboys can spot someone who lies to themselves from a mile away.
5. Your mind can be your best friend or your worst enemy. You get to decide.
6. Fucking is good but loving yourself is better.
7. "Money can't buy you class."—Countess Luanne
8. In a sea of red flags, you can either sink or swim. Grab your life vest and get the hell out of there, honey.
9. True passion is making someone (or yourself) a priority every day, not just when it's sexy.
10. Self-sabotage always starts with ignoring your intuition.
11. Look for the warning signs of a nonreciprocator way before you see them naked.
12. You are the love of your life. You are the true love you've been searching for.

What Does Self-Love Really Mean?

A few months before I wrote this chapter, I noticed some pain in the joints of my hand. It was getting worse, to the point that it was interfering with my day-to-day activities. I also noticed a rash on my skin. I didn't know for sure if these things were connected, but I thought it was time to see a doctor about these strange symptoms.

After a perfunctory exam, the doctor told me that my symptoms were due to my weight. "Don't you want to run any blood tests or anything?" I asked. He said it wouldn't be necessary and that I should notice an improvement if I go on a diet and lose some weight. Weight discrimination is a major problem in the medical field.

As a person who has done the work to educate myself about fatphobia, body acceptance, and eating disorders, I knew what this was. The doctor didn't bother with giving me a proper exam because he thought any health issues could be reduced to one thing, my larger-sized body. I immediately got a second opinion.

After some extensive blood work (that should have been done the first time), the second doctor told me that I had rheumatoid arthritis and needed to get on a treatment plan immediately. If I had listened to that other doctor and starved myself thinking that would make my symptoms disappear, the condition would have progressed, and I would be way worse than I am now. I loved myself enough to advocate for myself.

After my diagnosis, I was nervous to tell my partner out of fear that he was going to leave me. Rheumatoid arthritis is a lifelong disease that affects everyday life, and I was afraid it would be too much of a burden for him. But, in another act of self-love, I came clean and told my boyfriend, ready to face whatever his reaction would be. After a long talk, he offered me loving support and compassion. It was so freeing and truly made me realize how far I'd come, from fuckboys who didn't give a shit about me to a real partner who is supporting me through a chronic health condition. Thank the gay heavens I came up with that compatibility scale!

As the former mayor of Shitty Self-Esteem Town in Self-Sabotage County, I know a thing or two about the depths of self-hatred. But I'm grateful that I've explored those dark caverns within me so I can see how far I've come on the quest to love myself. But self-love doesn't mean self-perfection. Far from it.

Imagine someone you love dearly. Picture them in your mind. Do they have little quirks and imperfections that you love because it makes them uniquely them? Maybe they have a chipped tooth that makes their smile mischievous but warm. Perhaps they have this one hair that sticks up, no matter how much they try to comb it down. Or maybe they have a boisterous laugh that shakes the walls, but it fills the room with pure joy. Now take a look at yourself in the mirror. Notice all of the things that make you recognizable to those you love, including those beautifully perfect imperfections. Can you see them the way your loved ones see them?

When I do mirror and body work, I take in every aspect of myself. I look in the mirror every morning and tell my reflection all the things I like about myself. I like my hair, my body, my love handles, my smile. Even if I don't totally feel it in the moment, it's like muscle memory. The more I do it, the more I believe it. Self-love is a skill. Especially in a world that constantly reminds us how undesirable our human "flaws" are, we must practice loving and accepting ourselves every day. The best thing about this is, the more you practice loving the fuck out of yourself, the more desirable you become in the world.

According to the dictionary, *self-love* is defined as "an appreciation of one's own worth or virtue and proper regard for and attention to one's own happiness or well-being."[3] But what is the best way to pay attention to our happiness and well-being? The self-care industry is worth about $450 billion in the United States. I found this

---

3 *Merriam-Webster.com Dictionary*, s.v. "self-love," accessed February 11, 2024, https://www.merriam-webster.com/dictionary/self-love.

interesting because the diet industry in the US is worth about $75 billion. Here are these two industries with a complicated relationship, but both are profiting when we feel neglected and fat (according to biased body standards). So in a land where big companies stand to profit off us not loving ourselves, how do we resist? I believe it's by being kind to ourselves and letting that lead everything else we do in our lives. There was a powerful article about self-love in *Psychology Today* that stated, "To love yourself is not an act of selfishness, it is an act of kindness toward others because when you love yourself, others don't have to deal with your unresolved problems." The article went on to define four aspects of self-love:

1. Self-awareness—the ability to be in touch with your thoughts, feelings, triggers, and why you feel the way you do. Some call this emotional intelligence.
2. Self-worth—thinking negatively about ourselves is the fastest way to kill our self-worth. We build our self-worth when we believe that we deserve love and respect.
3. Self-esteem—when we have a high sense of self-worth, we will act accordingly. This is also known as self-esteem. When we have a high self-esteem, we have the audacity to strive for the lives we truly desire.
4. Self-care—despite what the self-care industry wants you to believe, self-care doesn't have to cost money. Sure, a massage feels great, but so does a walk in nature or having a cup of tea with a friend.

If I had to define self-love, it would be a full knowing and acceptance of myself in all of my imperfect, sometimes messy, fat or skinny, healthy or recovering, lonely, happy, sad, hilarious, horny, depressed, elated states. It's forgiveness for my mistakes and a willingness to let go of shame and grow into my strengths. It's allowing myself the space to feel everything that needs to be felt and allowing myself connection, even when it might be hard for me to believe I deserve it. It's building trust with myself by listening to my intuition. Above all, it's feeling at home with myself. What is your definition of self-love?

Here are a few prompts to get you started on defining self-love for you:

I love myself enough to _____.

I still need to work on _____.

I make my happiness a priority by _____.

I show myself gratitude when I _____.

To Me, with Love

If you could go back and talk to your younger self, what would you say? Would you warn them of the dangers ahead? Or would you celebrate their strength and courage? If there was one piece of wisdom you could offer to your younger self, what would it be? As I finished writing this book, the desire to write a letter to my younger self became overwhelming. There were things I wanted to say to the depressed and desperate version of myself that I found only after I'd gone through it all and looked back to see how, even though I was flawed, I was so incredibly lovable. I encourage you to write a letter to your younger self and keep the conversation going. There is no ally in the world like the most healed, wise, and compassionate version of ourselves. Here is mine. Thank you for taking this wild ride with me.

Dear Younger Me,

As I sit down to write this letter, a flood of memories and emotions wash over me. If I could turn back time and sit beside you, I would hold your hand, wipe away your tears, and whisper in your ear all the beautiful, wonderful things I've discovered about who we are. The road you're walking might seem treacherous and filled with pain, but I promise you, every step is worth it.

Remember those days when you'd come home from school, trying to swallow the stinging words and actions of bullies? Or the nights when you'd bury your face in the pillow, wishing to be anyone but you? I want you to know, young Ryan, that in the grand scheme of things, those tormentors will become mere footnotes in the epic tale of our life.

I know that the weight of hiding your sexuality feels crushing and the cloud of depression looms large; but with time, you will come to embrace, love, and celebrate that part of you. It's heart-wrenching to think of how deeply you doubt your worth, but that self-questioning is a phase that will pave the way to a profound self-awareness and acceptance.

The absence of our father was, and sometimes still is, a throbbing ache in our heart. While the sting of abandonment never truly disappears, it does transform. It becomes a testament to our resilience, our capacity to seek out and find love in a million other places, and our ability to be the father figure to ourselves that we never had.

It's going to take time, tears, and so much introspection, but one day, you will come to realize something beautiful: those parts of us that were ridiculed, shamed, and trampled upon?

They are your most radiant qualities. They are what make you unique, strong, and empathetic. They're sculpting you into the individual you will become—someone who knows the depth of pain but also the height of joy and love.

Had I known back then what I know now, perhaps the journey would have been easier. Perhaps I would have hugged myself a little tighter during those lonely nights or danced more freely during the days without fear of judgment. But every scar, every tear, every struggle was necessary. They are the building blocks of our character, the catalysts that push us to dig deep, find our strength, and discover the immense capacity of our heart to heal, love, and flourish.

So, dear younger me, while I wish I could shield you from the pain, I also cherish it. Because of those trying times, you will learn to appreciate the beauty in yourself and the world around you. It's because of the hurt that you will find strength. It's because of the darkness that you'll recognize the light.

Please know that you are loved, not just by the older me, but by countless souls you'll touch and inspire along the way. Your journey, though filled with trials, will be an incredible one, full of growth, love, and understanding. Keep that spark alive, and remember: every piece of you, even the parts you're not yet proud of, are the makings of a beautiful, remarkable human being. And if someone ever tries to put a crystal in your ass, run honey.

With the deepest love,
Your Older Self

Now it's your turn:

Dear Younger Self,

_____

_____

_____

_____

_____

_____

_____

_____

_____

_____

_____

_____

_____

_____

_____

_____

_____

_____

_____

_____

_____

_____

Love,

_____

A Note on Therapy

Throughout this book, I mention therapy quite a bit because it's been a big part of my healing and recovery process. I've been in some form of therapy since I was about eight years old. I've often joked that since I'm Jewish, it's a pretty typical thing for me to be in therapy for so many years. I've been so overly therapized that I sometimes overstep and find myself therapizing other people. Surprise, surprise, everyone hates that. Even though I joke that I'm overtherapized, I've learned and grown in ways that have improved my life exponentially.

So as your overtherapized friend, if you're thinking of finding a therapist, I highly suggest you find the right one specifically for your unique needs. For me, it was important that my therapist had expertise with eating disorders and OCD. I also prefer a gay man. It's hard to get a straight therapist to fully understand all the nuances and aspects of gay culture and relationships. For instance, I could tell that my straight therapist was horrified when I told her about the Fetishizer. But when I discussed it with my gay psychiatrist, he reassured me that fetishes were more common in the gay community. A gay therapist/psychiatrist is more likely to understand the things I've gone through as a gay kid and later as an adult trying to navigate the gay dating world. It's important for you to be clear on what you need from a therapist and then find someone who can meet your specific needs.

Oftentimes, it takes a few therapists before you find the right one. My method was to see a therapist three times before I decide if they are a good fit for me. If, in those three visits, I didn't feel like they could help me, I'd move on. Some people believe that they can get what they need in one or two sessions and that the work will be done for them. But the reality is, therapy is work, and it's often a long road. You'll want to find someone who you're comfortable with for the long haul. While you should feel comfortable with your therapist, you will likely be addressing uncomfortable topics together. The goal of therapy is to get relief from emotional suffering and other symptoms and to elevate your quality of life.

I've had many awakenings in therapy. But I never would have had those awakenings if I wasn't willing to dig through difficult memories and unhealthy coping mechanisms first. Not only has my life improved, but my relationships are better, especially my relationship with myself. The pain of the past is never fully gone, but I've learned to manage it, and most importantly, listen to it. I've spent so much of my life suffering. But in my healing process, I've learned to set down the resentment, which exacerbated my suffering. I've learned that life is too short to indulge in that suffering. It was there so I could learn the difficult lessons about being a gay man in a larger-size body, about overcoming abuse and an eating disorder, about finding love for myself in a place that's designed in so many ways to make me hate myself.

It's important to note that therapy and mental health services are not always accessible for everyone. There are some accessible resources at the end of this book for people who need support. Whatever you are experiencing, it's important to have the courage to reach out for support, whatever that looks like for you. We are not meant to do this alone.

A New Fuckboy Quiz

At the beginning of this book, I offered you a quiz to find out which fuckboy you're most attracted to. We laughed at all the hilariously disordered dudes with their sex crystals, their cringey fetishes, and their cocaine shits. We joked about how many red flags I blew past to put myself in the most awkward dating scenarios ever. We discussed the warning signs, the Trauma Divas, and the tired intuition queen who just wants us to stop sabotaging ourselves. But now that we've been through it all together, I want to offer you a final quiz:

Ready?

> Question one:
> If you truly love yourself completely and unconditionally, who would your ideal partner be?

That's it. That's the whole quiz. My hope for you is to see that if you truly love yourself completely and unconditionally, you already have your ideal partner: *you.* But the amazing part is, once you are so full of love for yourself that it radiates out of your pores and shines on people in your atmosphere, you will attract a partner who is capable of loving you the way you love yourself. It's a kind of love magic that even the most sordid swamps of those dating apps can't penetrate (pun intended!).

FUCKBOY LESSON *Number Twelve*

> You are the love of your life. You are the
> true love you've been searching for.

WE'RE ALL DIAMONDS

I heard someone say once that the brightest diamonds are forged under immense pressure. With everything I've endured, from my childhood to my adult life, especially as a gay man with an eating disorder, I've certainly experienced immense pressure. It was painful and intense and heartbreaking and scary and exhilarating. I had no idea that the strongest gem in the world, my true, beautiful inner self, was being forged. To be a human being in these difficult times means to be under immense pressure, all of us. So that means we are all the brightest diamonds. And as Stella Starlight (a.k.a., my intuition) would say, "Remember who you are, gorgeous! Get out there and shine! But don't do any stupid shit while you're out there."

Okay, do I wish that I didn't experience some of those things? Absolutely. Trust me, I could have done without the chlamydia, the cocaine shits, the injuries, and the crystals, but without all of those crazy stories, we wouldn't have had this time together. Those stories are mine. They belong to me, no matter how cringey or embarrassing.

My hope is that in reading this book, you've been able to accept the vulnerable, embarrassing, heartbreaking things about your own story. Because all of the parts of your story matter, even the ones you wish you could forget. They matter because your pain matters, your joy matters, and your self-love and acceptance matter most of all. They are what make you a rare, precious, and beautiful diamond.

And I know you will find someone who loves to see you shine.

ACKNOWLEDGMENTS

To my mom, Shelby, and Brooke—your constant acceptance and embrace have been my guiding lights through every chapter of my life. Your love has given me strength and courage beyond measure.

Jared, my beloved partner—thank you for not only listening to my story but also for giving me the space to share it. With you, I've learned the true meaning of love, and for that, I am endlessly grateful.

Jamie and Kristen—your belief in me and my story has been a constant source of encouragement. Your support has given me the confidence to share my experiences with the world.

To my faithful companion and fur baby, Riley—your presence has taught me the boundless depths of unconditional love. Your loyalty has been a constant source of comfort and joy.

And to all the fuckboys I used to love—though our paths may have diverged, you've each played a part in shaping my journey. Through heartache and growth, I've found the strength to write these pages.

To everyone who has touched my life, whether briefly or profoundly, thank you for being a part of my story.

With love and gratitude,
Ryan

SUPPORT AND RESOURCES

National Eating Disorders Association
www.nationaleatingdisorders.org

Eating Disorder Hope:
www.eatingdisorderhope.com

Anorexia Nervosa & Associated Disorders (ANAD) Hotline:
1-888-375-7767
www.anad.org

Alliance for Eating Disorder Awareness Helpline
1-866-662-1235
www.allianceforeatingdisorders.com

National Suicide Prevention Lifeline
1-800-273-TALK (8255)

Suicide and Crisis Lifeline
988

Crisis Text Line
Text "HELLO" to 741741

Substance Abuse and Mental Health Services Administration (SAMHSA)
1-800-662-HELP (4357)
www.samhsa.gov/find-help/national-helpline
www.findtreatment.gov

LGBTQ+ National Hotline
  1-888-843-4564

It Gets Better
  www.itgetsbetter.org

The Trevor Project
  www.thetrevorproject.org

Project Heal
  www.theprojectheal.org

Mental Health America
  www.mhanational.org

Alcoholics Anonymous
  www.aa.org

Al-Anon
  www.al-anon.org

Domestic Violence Hotline
  1-800-799-SAFE (7233)

BIBLIOGRAPHY

Baer, Drake, and Allana Akhtar. "11 Scientific Reasons Why Attractive People Are More Successful in Life." *Business Insider*, November 10, 2014. https://www.businessinsider.com/beautiful-people-make-more-money-2014-11.

Coduto, Kathryn D., Roselyn J. Lee-Won, and Young Min Baek. "Swiping for Trouble: Problematic Dating Application Use Among Psychologically Distraught Individuals and the Paths to Negative Outcomes." *Sage Journals*, July 3, 2019. https://journals.sagepub.com/doi/10.1177/0265407519861153.

DiDonato, Theresa E. "We All Want Passion. But Do We Need It? *Psychology Today*. October 10, 2014. https://www.psychologytoday.com/us/blog/meet-catch-and-keep/201410/we-all-want-passion-do-we-need-it.

"Eating Disorders in Males." *Eating Disorder Hope*, December 14, 2023. https://www.eatingdisorderhope.com/risk-groups/men.

"Eating Disorder Statistics." ANAD (National Association of Anorexia Nervosa and Associated Disorders). January 11, 2024. https://anad.org/eating-disorder-statistic/.

"Eating Disorder Statistics." National Eating Disorders Association, January 8, 2024. https://www.nationaleatingdisorders.org/statistics/.

Emamzadeh, Arash. "What Is Love Addiction?" *Psychology Today*, February 10, 2019. https://www.psychologytoday.com/us/blog/finding-new-home/201902/what-is-love-addiction.

"Emotional Fatigue and Burnout in Online Dating—Data Study." *Singles Reports*, April 18, 2022. https://singlesreports.com/reports/emotional -fatigue-or-burnout-in-online- dating/#methodology.

"Everything You Need to Know About Exposure and Response Prevention Therapy." McLean Hospital, June 8, 2023. https://www.mcleanhospital.org /essential/erp#:~:text=What%20Is%20Exposure%20and%20Response ,remove%20distressing%20situations%20and%20thoughts.

Faden, Justin, Jonathan Levin, Ronak Mistry, and Jessica Wang. "Delusional Disorder, EROTOMANIC Type, Exacerbated by Social Media Use." *Case Reports in Psychiatry*. March 7, 2017. https://www.ncbi.nlm.nih.gov/pmc /articles/PMC5359441.

Ferriss, Tim, and Brené Brown. "Brené Brown—Striving Versus Self-Acceptance, Saving Marriages, and More." *The Tim Ferriss Show*. YouTube, February 6, 2020. https://www.youtube.com/watch?v=Wh5SUF0gPWQ.

Grinspoon, Peter. "How to Recognize and Tame Your Cognitive Distortions." *Harvard Health*, May 4, 2022. https://www.health.harvard.edu/blog /how-to-recognize-and-tame-your-cognitive-distortions-202205042738.

"How Marriage Has Changed Over Centuries." *The Week*, June 1, 2012. https://theweek.com/articles/475141/how-marriage-changed-over -centuries.

Kaplan, Ilana. "DJ Khaled Said He Does Not Perform Oral Sex on Women Because 'There Are Different Rules for Men.'" *The Independent*, May 7, 2018. https://www.independent.co.uk/arts-entertainment/music/news /dj-khaled-the-breakfast-club-oral-sex-interview-2015-a8337276.html.

Khan, Arman. "What Falling for 'Fuckboys' Says About Your Attachment Style." *VICE*, November 10, 2022. https://www.vice.com/en/article/z34key /fuckboys-love-sex-dating-relationships-attachment-style.

LaMotte, Sandee. "Are You in Love or Just High on Chemicals in Your Brain? Answer: YES." CNN, February 14, 2020. https://edition.cnn.com/2020 /02/14/health/brain-on-love-wellness/index.html.

Mellody, Pia, Andrea Wells Miller, and Keith Miller. *Facing Love Addiction: Giving Yourself the Power to Change the Way You Love.* New York: HarperOne, 2010.

Migliore, Lauren. "In Love with Love: The Science of Love Addiction." *Brain World*, February 13, 2022. https://brainworldmagazine.com/love-love -science-love-addiction/#:~:text=It%E2%80%99s%20an%20experience %20of%20feeling,biological%20anthropologist%20at%20Rutgers%20 University.

Moore, Marissa. "OCD and Limerence: What Are Person-Focused Obsessions?" Psych Central, August 23, 2021. https://psychcentral.com /ocd/ocd-and-obsessive-thoughts-about-another-person#person-focused -obsessions.

Morissette, Alanis. "Podcast Episode 16: Pia Mellody." Alanis Morissette. November 29, 2019. https://alanis.com/news/podcast-episode-16-pia -mellody/.

Mutiwasekwa, Sarah-Len. "Self-Love." *Psychology Today*, November 12, 2019. https://www.psychologytoday.com/us/blog/the-upside-things/201911 /self-love.

Novotney, Amy. "What Happens in Your Brain When You're in Love?" American Psychological Association, February 10, 2023. https://www.apa .org/topics/marriage-relationships/brain-on-love.

Nuth, Grace. "The Troubadour's Guide to Modern Courtly Love." *Enchanted Living Magazine.* December 27, 2017. https://enchantedlivingmagazine .com/troubadours-guide-modern-courtly-love/.

"Obsessive-Compulsive." Mental Health Foundation, May 26, 2023. https:// mentalhealthfoundation.org/health-conditions/anxiety-disorders /obsessive-compulsive/.

"Self-Care Trends." IRI. Accessed January 19, 2024. https://www.circana.com /intelligence/reports/2024/examine-the-self-care-opportunity/.

Swanner, Nate. "Ghosting, Orbiting, Breadcrumbing, and Other Modern Relationship Terms Explained." The Manual, September 30, 2021. https:// www.themanual.com/culture/modern-relationship-terms-explained/.

Tull, Matthew. "Factors Associated With Risk-Taking Behaviors." Verywell Mind. November 21, 2023. https://www.verywellmind.com/risk-taking -2797384.

Turban, Jack. "We Need to Talk About How Grindr Is Affecting Gay Men's Mental Health." Vox. April 4, 2018. https://www.vox.com/science-and -health/2018/4/4/17177058/grindr-gay-men-mental-health-psychiatrist.

"United States Weight Loss & Diet Control Market." Research and Markets. March 2023. https://www.businesswire.com/news/home/20230505005 166/en/United-States-Weight-Loss-Diet-Control-Market-Report-2023 -The-75-Billion-Market-Grew-Nearly-15-in-2022-from-the-Depressed -Level-of-2020---ResearchAndMarkets.com.

Welch, Ashley. "Study Seeks Answers to the 'Orgasm Gap.'" CBS News, March 2, 2017. https://www.cbsnews.com/news/orgasm-gap-sex-study -straight-women-have-fewer-orgasms-than-men/.

"What Is Happiness?" *Psychology Today.* Accessed January 19, 2024. https:// www.psychologytoday.com/us/basics/happiness.

Wu, Katherine. "Love, Actually: The Science Behind Lust, Attraction, and Companionship." Science in the News, June 19, 2020. https://sitn.hms .harvard.edu/flash/2017/love-actually-science-behind-lust-attraction -companionship/.

ABOUT THE AUTHOR

RYAN SHELDON is a renowned speaker, brawn model, and fervent advocate for eating disorder awareness and self-love. He has appeared on prominent media outlets such as *The Today Show*, BBC, Huffington Post, and *Teen Vogue*, and passionately addresses body image, self-acceptance, and self-esteem in high schools. He has also cohosted a weekly radio segment on *Loveline* with Dr. Chris Donaghue, focusing on body image issues and inspiring young adults with discussions about masculinity, identity, and body confidence.

Sheldon's message is one of resilience as he confronts weight-bullying and openly shares his struggles with binge eating disorder while exploring his evolving sexuality. He served as the chair of the ambassador program at the National Eating Disorders Association and has been on billboards in Times Square as a brawn model for prestigious brands, including Hanes Underwear, Bonobos, and Target. His chapter in the book *Eating Disorders Don't Discriminate: Stories of Illness, Hope and Recovery from Diverse Voices* offers guidance and hope to those on a similar journey. In addition to his advocacy and media work, Sheldon finds solace in the company of his beloved dog, Riley, and the world of music at the piano. Ryan Sheldon's Instagram, @realryansheldon, continues to be a platform for spreading messages of self-love, acceptance, and empowerment, making him an inspiring guide for others on their path to healing and self-discovery.